· THE ·

WALT DISNEY WORLD®
TRIVIA BOOK
VOLUME 2

More Secrets, History and Fun Facts
Behind the Magic

Louis A. Mongello

The Walt Disney World® Trivia Book Volume 2:
More Secrets, History and Fun Facts Behind the Magic

Published by The Intrepid Traveler, P.O. Box 531, Branford, CT 06405
http://www.intrepidtraveler.com

ISBN-13: 978-1-887140-63-8
Library of Congress Control Number: 2003114403

Book Jacket: George Foster, Foster & Foster, Inc.
Interior Book Design: Ellen Lytle, City Design

Printed in the United States of America

10 9 8 7 6 5 4 3

Copyrights, Trademarks, Etc.

This book makes reference to various Disney copyrighted characters, trademarks, marks, and registered marks owned by The Walt Disney Company and Disney Enterprises, Inc. All references to these properties, and to The Twilight Zone®, a registered trademark of CBS, Inc., are made solely for editorial purposes. Neither the author nor the publisher makes any commercial claim to their use, and neither is affiliated with either The Walt Disney Company or CBS, Inc. in any way.

This book is UNAUTHORIZED and UNOFFICIAL. It has not been reviewed by The Walt Disney Company and is not in any way authorized by, endorsed by, or associated with it or with any of its corporate sponsors or affiliates. The author simply wants to share the Walt Disney World® Resort (WDW) expertise he has gained through years of research, visiting the parks, and collecting Disney memorabilia with other WDW fans in hopes of enhancing their love and enjoyment of this very special place.

Photo Credits

Cover photo: Louis A. Mongello
Interior photos: Bride, page 204 © Gerard Photography Inc.
People, pages iii, v, vii, viii, 12, and 205 © Louis A. Mongello.
Abraham Lincoln, Theodore Roosevelt, and Mark Twain courtesy of the Library of Congress.
All other interior photos are protected under copyright by the individual photographers and licensed for use through iStockphoto.com and Photos.com.

About the Author

Louis A. Mongello has been fascinated by the Walt Disney World® Resort (WDW) since his first visit at the age of three, when WDW and the Magic Kingdom were just over a month old. Since then, he has visited on dozens of occasions, each one more enjoyable than the last. He has also endeavored to learn everything he can about this magical place, assembling a vast array of Walt Disney World® memorabilia in the process. His ever-growing collection includes rare documents outlining Walt Disney's original plans for his Florida project, books, articles, photos, videos, park merchandise from days gone by, and almost anything with the words "Walt Disney World" on it. Every visit continues to be a learning experience for him, as his passion for WDW parallels his desire to learn more about it.

By sharing his "useless knowledge" of WDW's history, secrets, and treasures with you, Louis hopes this book will add extra magic to your own visits, as well as bring the magic home for you. He believes that you will have as much fun reading the book as he did researching and writing it. He also hopes that it will spark your interest in what makes the magic really happen.

Louis' other interests include poker, computers, travel, and just spending time with family. He holds a bachelor's degree in Sociology from Villanova University and received a Juris Doctor from Seton Hall University School of Law in 1994. After serving as law clerk to the Presiding Judge of the largest vicinage in the nation, he practiced law actively for nine years. During that time, he formed and managed a computer consulting and web development firm for small businesses. Today, he is the Chief Technology Officer and Director of Operations for medical imaging centers located throughout New Jersey. He still doesn't know what he wants to be when he grows up.

Louis lives in Florida, with his wife Deanna, daughter Marion Rose (whose face graces the cover of this book), and son Nicolas Peter.

Dedication

This book, and everything that has come from it, would never have been possible without the love, support, and understanding of my family.

To my wife, whose infinite patience and encouragement go beyond anything that I could have imagined: Thank you for your inspiration, vision, and enduring support. I never could have done this without you by my side. You define the words "soul mate" and help me always to become a better man and father. You continue to amaze me on a daily basis in everything that you say, do, and feel. I am who I am today because of you.

To my children, who have given me a new outlook on life and an appreciation for so many things that I never could have had without you: We waited a long time for you, and you were both worth waiting for. This is just the beginning of our making memories together.

To my brother, who has shared with me so many good times and bad (as well as monorail rides): You are both my trusted friend and someone I know will always be there for me. We'll always be kids at heart.

To my parents: I cannot give you enough thanks. You have given me more than words can express, far beyond the substantive and educational. I have learned more about love, life, and family from you than you can ever know. I hope I have made you proud.

Louis A. Mongello

Acknowledgements

I could not have created this book without the many individuals who helped along the way. I thank my entire family, who have always been there for me and given me reason to smile, along with the many other people who have accompanied me on this journey and whose support made this second book possible.

I also thank Sally Scanlon and Kelly Monaghan, my editor and publisher, for not only taking a chance with me and Volume 1 but also quickly becoming cherished friends. Thank you for letting me enjoy this incredible "E-ticket" ride. I hope it never ends.

To my friends and extended family at DisneyWorldTrivia.com, I never imagined that our small message forum would grow so quickly, yet still remain the friendly community that it is today. Thank you for your support, assistance, and everything else you do to make our site a place so many people call "home." I consider every member a part of my extended family, and there are many of you with whom I have made friendships I never could have imagined. I hate to mention names, for fear of omission, but I have to give special thanks to: Valerie (LC) — you have been with me from the very beginning, unwavering in your support, loyalty, and kindness; I can't say enough about what you have grown to mean to me and the community. Pat, we seemed to become friends overnight, as have our families; thanks for all you continue to do. Thank you, Nathan, for the friendship you and your family have extended to me and mine; "see you in another life, brother." To all of you whom I consider close friends — I hope you know who you are and understand why I can't name each of you here. To the Staff and each and every member who contributes in so many ways to the site — it is all that it is because of you.

To the countless dreamers and doers at the Walt Disney Company, including the Imagineers and Cast Members who clearly love what they do and bring the magic to so many people each and every day.

And to you, reader, for joining me in savoring the innocent feeling of being a kid again as you enter the Magic Kingdom. I am truly blessed to be able to share my love of WDW with you. We all "get it" as I like to say; so c'mon . . . let's have some fun together!

Table of Contents

INTRODUCTION

"When I get home, I shall write a book about this place."
– Alice in Wonderland

I never planned to write a book about Walt Disney World — let alone two books! People ask me all the time how the first book came to be, especially now that I've written a second one. To be honest, my route was circuitous. My parents took me for the first (of many) visits to Walt Disney World when I was three. My father took a photo of me, bad hair and all, on the curb of Main Street, U.S.A. in a place, which has come to be known affectionately as "The Spot," and from that moment on, I was hooked. For years, the joke in my family was that during our subsequent visits, I either entertained or bored them by spouting WDW facts and trivia as we walked the parks.

I had always said that I wished I could do something with all the "useless knowledge" I had floating around in my head. Then one evening, when I was looking for my next project, the idea of writing a book came to mind. What could I possibly write about? I wasn't interested in writing about the law (my vocation at the time), and I didn't think I could write adequately about computers or technology (my other profession at the time). So, what else did I know something about . . . that really interested me? Well . . . I knew a bit about Walt Disney World.

My mind started racing and the process began. I checked and was amazed to discover that no book devoted to WDW trivia existed. Now I was a man on a mission. I started to write down (OK, type) things I knew off the top of my head and then tried to create what I hoped would be some interesting questions and answers. "Slow down, Lou; are you sure this is a good idea?" I asked myself. Who better to solicit for an honest answer than my wife? I went upstairs and hemmed and hawed my way into telling her my idea. In typical Deanna fashion, she immediately supported it and brainstormed with me, and my quest to write a WDW trivia book was officially born.

In an effort to do it "right" the first time out, I gave myself a quick and dirty lesson in getting a book published. While the option of self-publishing was available to me, I challenged myself to find a publisher that would take me and my book on the journey together. I was warned that my quest would be long, frustrating, and test the limits of my ego. Long story short (too late), after receiving more rejection letters than I care to discuss, I got a phone call from Kelly Monaghan, Publisher of The Intrepid Traveler, the company that publishes Steven Barrett's Hidden Mickeys book. I had a feeling that they might just be the perfect fit. Little did I know how right I would be! My wife, who answered Kelly's call, came running down the stairs to get me. Kelly and I spoke for some time, and a few weeks later, while vacationing with my family, I signed a contract. As we sat at dinner celebrating, I quickly realized, "Hey! Now I gotta WRITE this thing!"

I spent the next few months literally locked in my basement office every night, researching and writing furiously until about 3:30 a.m. My wife, pregnant, patient, and more understanding than I could ever have hoped for, supported me throughout the process. She encouraged me to continue working even after our first child was born — on Mickey's 75th birthday (our baby knew what she was getting into)!

In fact, my entire family was excited about what I was working on. We are a family of Disney fans, and my research and writing stirred countless memories of our times together at WDW. It made me realize that in addition to all the things Disney and the Cast Members do to make every Guest feel special and have an unforgettable experience, the most potent "magic" of a WDW visit lies in making memories with family and friends.

What makes WDW itself so special for me lies in the details — an attraction's story, a small prop, a cleverly disguised homage to a former attraction, an unexpected surprise. These are the things that separate Walt Disney World from every other place on Earth, and yet these details are often overlooked. This book is designed to help you discover and enjoy them.

About the Book and Its Format

Readers often tell me that they use Volume 1 as a game, quizzing each other around the table or on the drive to and from Disney World. That's exactly how I hoped it would be used. In fact, I wrote in trivia format because I wanted readers to use my book to play with family and friends, and I also wanted them to be able to pick it up, open it to any page, and enjoy a fun fact without having to read a narrative from beginning to end. My hope is that the book will inspire you to visit WDW and take the book along with you. I think you'll really have fun and, at the same time, enhance and appreciate the "magic" a little more.

While there is no way to cover everything that Walt Disney World has to offer in a book, I've tried to take you around "the World" with me to see as much as we can together. The first chapter explores some WDW history and little-known facts and gives you an opportunity to see how well you know some of the attractions. Each of the following four chapters covers a single theme park, so you can easily follow along as you tour the park. The sixth and final trivia chapter explores WDW beyond the theme parks, from Downtown Disney, to the resorts, restaurants, monorail, and more.

If you're looking for a specific topic or attraction, check the Index. If you're looking for even more WDW trivia — along with games, articles, vacation planning, audio/video downloads, photos, and more, visit www.DisneyWorldTrivia.com and become part of our friendly online community, which we affectionately call the "Happiest Forums on Earth."

About Names

Over time, many park and attraction names and naming styles have changed. For example, when Epcot opened it was called "EPCOT Center." Its name was later changed to "EPCOT," and then to "Epcot." Unless the question relates specifically to an earlier stage or version of a park or attraction, I have used the current name. Also, in the interests of space, many names are spelled out in full only the first time they are mentioned and shortened after that. For example, Walt Disney World® Resort may become WDW, *Rock 'n' Roller Coaster Starring Aerosmith* may become *Rock 'n' Roller Coaster*.

Accuracy and Other Impossible Dreams

All facts and statistics are accurate as we go to press. But WDW is constantly changing. So you may want to check my web site, www.DisneyWorldTrivia.com, for updates. If you have questions, comments, or suggestions — or notice that I've missed something, you can let me know by emailing me personally at lou@disneyworldtrivia.com.

I sincerely thank all of you who enjoyed Volume 1 and took the time to let me know; it is your support that led to this second volume. Your appreciation means more to me than you'll ever know. I hope you enjoy reading Volume 2 as much as I enjoyed writing it.

Did You Know?

3,000,000 CHOCOLATE-COVERED MICKEY MOUSE
ICE CREAM BARS ARE SOLD EVERY YEAR AT WDW.

CHAPTER ONE

All Around The 'World'

1. Where was an apartment built for Walt Disney's family?
- a.) Inside Cinderella Castle
- b.) Above one of the shops on Main Street, U.S.A.
- c.) Above the Firehouse on Main Street, U.S.A.
- d.) In a building on a service road between Disney's Contemporary Resort and the Magic Kingdom

2. What was formally announced to the public on June 5, 1995?
- a.) The closing of *20,000 Leagues Under the Sea*
- b.) Disney's Wild Animal Kingdom
- c.) Disney's Millennium Celebration
- d.) Disney's Wide World of Sports Complex

3. On what date was WDW's dedication broadcast on national TV?
- a.) October 1, 1971
- b.) October 25, 1971
- c.) October 29, 1971
- d.) It was never broadcast on TV.

4. Which park is home to WDW's tallest "mountain"?
- a.) Magic Kingdom
- b.) Epcot
- c.) Disney's Animal Kingdom
- d.) The Studios

Did You Know?

THE FOUR OFFICIAL WALT DISNEY WORLD COLORS ARE LAGOON BLUE, MINT GREEN, PUMPKIN ORANGE, AND LAVENDER.

5. Where can you find Cousin Elrod?
- a.) *Big Thunder Mountain Railroad*
- b.) *Carousel of Progress*
- c.) *Horizons*
- d.) *Country Bear Jamboree*

6. What is the name of Disney's complimentary service that transports Guests and their luggage from Orlando International Airport to WDW?
- a.) Magic Journeys
- b.) Disney's Magical Gatherings
- c.) DreamFlight
- d.) Disney's Magical Express

7. How many miles of drainage canals are there on WDW property?
- a.) 4.3
- b.) 43
- c.) 430
- d.) 6

8. Where could you hear, "And now, as long as you're all standing . . . we have a wonderful magic trick for you"?
- a.) *The Enchanted Tiki Room – Under New Management*
- b.) *The Timekeeper*
- c.) *Ellen's Energy Adventure*
- d.) *Jim Henson's MuppetVision 3-D*

9. What did the Department of Defense do with Disney in February 1994?

- a.) Assisted in designing security checkpoints in backstage areas
- b.) Leased the entire Disney Inn Resort
- c.) Placed undercover officers throughout the parks to counter potential terrorism
- d.) Provided Imagineers with technology used in creating *Test Track*

10. WDW is the second leading purchaser in the U.S. of ___?
- a.) Popcorn
- b.) Paint
- c.) Laundry detergent
- d.) Explosives

11. Who appeared on the first Disney Dollars $10 bill?
- a.) Donald
- b.) Mickey
- c.) Goofy
- d.) Minnie

12. Where could you hear, "For your own safety, please grip your armrests firmly"?
- a.) *It's Tough to be a Bug!*
- b.) *The ExtraTERRORestrial Alien Encounter*
- c.) *Jim Henson's MuppetVision 3-D*
- d.) *Sci-Fi Dine-In Theater*

13. What did Walt Disney call a "timeless land of enchantment"?
- a.) Fantasyland
- b.) Tomorrowland

c.) Adventureland

d.) The Magic Kingdom

14. Which attraction was brought to WDW from Disneyland Paris as part of the Disneyland 50th Anniversary Celebration?
a.) *Soarin'*
b.) *Lights, Motors, Action!*
c.) *Cinderellabration*
d.) Lucky the dinosaur

15. Where will you find the Torre del Cielo?
a.) Mexico pavilion
b.) Pecos Bill Café
c.) El Pirate Y El Périco
d.) *Pirates of the Caribbean*

16. The first large parcel of land used for WDW was purchased from whom?
a.) An Orange county resident
b.) A Florida state senator
c.) The state of Florida
d.) Busch Gardens

17. "Attention. All visitors from Galaxy Planetary One, please keep all horns, claws, and tentacles clear of oncoming Metroliner Vehicles" can be heard in ___?
a.) *Buzz Lightyear's Space Ranger Spin*
b.) *Star Tours*
c.) *Tomorrowland Transit Authority*
d.) *Stitch's Great Escape*

18. What show is presented in the Hollywood Hills Amphitheater?
a.) *Fantasmic!*
b.) *IllumiNations*
c.) *"Beauty and the Beast" – Live on Stage*
d.) *Indiana Jones Epic Stunt Spectacular*

19. Which of these celebrities was NOT featured in the NBC broadcast of the dedication of WDW?
a.) Bob Hope
b.) Jonathan Winters
c.) Bobby Unser
d.) Jimmy Stewart

20. Where can you find the Olympiad Health Club?
a.) Contemporary Resort
b.) Disney-MGM Studios
c.) All-Star Sports Resort
d.) Wide World of Sports

21. When WDW was built, Bay Lake was stocked with how many fish?
a.) None
b.) 700
c.) 7,000
d.) 70,000

22. Who is the official mascot of Disney's Environmentality program?
a.) Mickey
b.) Jiminy Cricket
c.) Pinocchio
d.) Pluto

23. What attraction in WDW was the first to include live animals?
a.) *Jungle Cruise*
b.) *20,000 Leagues Under the Sea*
c.) *The Living Seas*
d.) *Kilimanjaro Safaris*

24. In Walt's original vision of Epcot as a working city, how many permanent residents did he anticipate?
a.) 500
b.) 2,000
c.) 20,000
d.) 200,000

25. When did WDW introduce the FASTPASS ticketing system?
a.) 1989
b.) 1995
c.) 1999
d.) 2001

26. Where could you hear, "Flash photography? I wouldn't. It alters the homing signal and that's not good"?
a.) *The ExtraTERRORestrial Alien Encounter*
b.) *DINOSAUR*
c.) *Body Wars*
d.) *Star Tours*

27. You'll find the Carthay Circle Theater in ___ ?
a.) Disney-MGM Studios
b.) Downtown Disney
c.) Disney's Animal Kingdom
d.) World Showcase

28. What character was created for the Florida Citrus Growers when they sponsored *Tropical Serenade*?
a.) Ollie The Orange
b.) The Orange Bird
c.) Citrus Sammy
d.) Tommy The Tangerine Tiki Bird

29. Where would you find Doubloon Lagoon?
a.) *Pirates of the Caribbean*
b.) Caribbean Beach Resort
c.) Port Orleans Resort – French Quarter
d.) Typhoon Lagoon

30. Why was the Buena Vista Construction Company formed?
a.) To build attraction show buildings
b.) It was a fake name used to purchase some of the land for WDW.
c.) To design and build roads around the WDW property
d.) To complete construction of one of the resorts

31. Which of the following was WDW the first to install in the U.S.?
a.) A monorail system
b.) A pneumatic trash collection system
c.) A Circle-Vision 360 film
d.) A PeopleMover

32. Where are you invited to "Open Your Eyes to the World Around You"?
   a.) Rafiki's Planet Watch
   b.) Innoventions
   c.) Main Street, U.S.A.
   d.) Entrance to World Showcase

33. What was the *Backstage Magic* show?
   a.) A magic show on Main Street, U.S.A.
   b.) Epcot show about computers
   c.) A behind-the-scenes tour of the Magic Kingdom
   d.) An improv show that played near the *Backstage Tour* ride in the Studios

34. How many Circle-Vision films are currently playing at WDW?

   a.) 0
   b.) 1
   c.) 2
   d.) 3

35. At what attraction's exit can you find a sign that reads, "May all your adventures be long-lasting"?
   a.) *Honey, I Shrunk the Audience*
   b.) *Star Tours*
   c.) *Indiana Jones Epic* stunt show
   d.) *Kali River Rapids*

36. Where could you hear, "you may not survive to pass this way again"?
   a.) *Pirates of the Caribbean*
   b.) *Maelstrom*
   c.) *The Great Movie Ride*
   d.) *The Haunted Mansion*

37. You'll find Ursus R. Bear in or on ___?
   a.) *Pangani Forest Exploration-Trail*
   b.) Wilderness Lodge
   c.) Pecos Bill Café
   d.) *Country Bear Jamboree*

38. What has been considered the most complicated piece of show equipment ever built by Walt Disney Imagineering?
   a.) "Hopper" from *It's Tough to be a Bug!*
   b.) The special effects used in *Fantasmic!*
   c.) The Earth Globe used in

IllumiNations: Reflections of Earth

d.) The Yeti Audio-Animatronics for *Expedition Everest*

39. Where can you find "Dave V. Jones Mine"?

a.) *The Living Seas*

b.) *Pirates of the Caribbean*

c.) Yacht Club Resort

d.) *Big Thunder Mountain Railroad*

40. Who offers sailing lessons in WDW?

a.) Pirate Goofy

b.) Captain Hook

c.) Admiral Joe Fowler

d.) Roy E. Disney

41. Which of the following attractions did NOT involve a partnership with film director (ever see *Star Wars*?) George Lucas?

a.) *The ExtraTERRORestrial Alien Encounter*

b.) *Indiana Jones Epic* stunt show

c.) *Twilight Zone Tower of Terror*

d.) *Captain EO*

42. What is "Imaginum"?

a.) A former performance group

b.) The material that covers the outside of the buildings in Animal Kingdom's Africa

c.) The fictional material used in *Journey Into Your Imagination* to create "Figment"

d.) A snack shop in the Studios

43. Where would you head to find Schweitzer Falls?

a.) Typhoon Lagoon

b.) *Splash Mountain*

c.) Germany pavilion

d.) *Jungle Cruise*

44. Where could you hear, "Four forward. Four forward. Adjusting to the right a little"?

a.) *The American Adventure*

b.) *Mission: SPACE*

c.) *Spaceship Earth*

d.) *Body Wars*

45. What name was originally proposed for *The Great Movie Ride*?

a.) *The Magic of Movies*

b.) *Hooray for Hollywood!*

c.) *Great Moments at the Movies*

d.) *Backlot Magic*

46. In which attraction is the "Inventor of the Year Award" handed out?

a.) *Honey, I Shrunk the Audience*

b.) *Journey Into Imagination with Figment*

c.) *Carousel of Progress*

d.) *Jim Henson's MuppetVision 3-D*

47. Bunny, Bubbles, and Beulah can be found in ___?

a.) *Country Bear Jamboree*

b.) *Jim Henson's MuppetVision 3-D*

c.) *Food Rocks*

d.) *The Great Movie Ride*

48. Where can you find a building inspired by the famous Castillo del Morro fort in San Juan, Puerto Rico?
- a.) Coronado Springs Resort
- b.) *Pirates of the Caribbean*
- c.) Mexico pavilion in Epcot
- d.) *Indiana Jones Epic* stunt show

49. Which of these classic TV game shows was filmed at WDW from 1990 to 1991?
- a.) *Let's Make a Deal*
- b.) *Family Feud*
- c.) *Joker's Wild*
- d.) *Hollywood Squares*

50. Who won the first WDW professional golf tournament?
- a.) Tiger Woods
- b.) Jack Nicklaus
- c.) Davis Love
- d.) Nick Price

51. WDW's Team Disney building is home to the world's largest ___?
- a.) Statue of Mickey Mouse
- b.) Collection of Disney memorabilia
- c.) Sundial
- d.) Employee cafeteria

52. Where could you hear, "Bake mode complete. Enjoy your meal"?
- a.) *Food Rocks*
- b.) *Carousel of Progress*
- c.) *Kitchen Kabaret*
- d.) *Living with the Land*

Did You Know?

WDW HAS OVER 2,000 ACRES OF GRASS TO MOW. THAT'S ABOUT 450,000 MOWING MILES ANNUALLY, OR 18 TRIPS AROUND THE EARTH'S EQUATOR, ASSUMING YOU MOW THREE TIMES A WEEK AS DISNEY DOES. (AND YOU COMPLAIN ABOUT MOWING YOUR LAWN!)

53. The Iron Spike Room is located in the ___?
- a.) Adventurers Club
- b.) Main Street, U.S.A. railroad station
- c.) Wilderness Lodge
- d.) *Big Thunder Mountain Railroad*

54. On which of these attractions do you NOT ride with a live Cast Member?
- a.) *Living with the Land*
- b.) *The Great Movie Ride*
- c.) *Jungle Cruise*
- d.) *Universe of Energy*

55. What emergency procedure was used for the first time in the State of Florida by WDW?
- a.) Putting laptop computers in security vehicles
- b.) The 911 phone system
- c.) An ambulatory helicopter
- d.) Using Pixie Dust in complicated surgical procedures

56. Where can you hear, "It's a glorious three-hour finale"?
- a.) *Jim Henson's MuppetVision 3-D*
- b.) *it's a small world*
- c.) *The Making of Me*
- d.) *Goofy About Health*

57. Who or what is the "importer of exotic gifts from the four corners of the globe"?
- a.) Sid Cahuenga's One of a Kind Shop

- b.) Shrunken Ned
- c.) The Zanzibar Trading Co.
- d.) Cornelius Coot

58. You'd find Captain Braddock in or on ___?
- a.) *Liberty Square Riverboat*
- b.) *Body Wars*
- c.) *Voyage of the Little Mermaid*
- d.) *Tom Sawyer Island*

59. "I was born modest, but it didn't last" can be heard in ___?
- a.) *The American Adventure*
- b.) *Legend of the Lion King*
- c.) *It's Tough to be a Bug!*
- d.) *Liberty Square Riverboat*

60. What was the name of the WDW nature park that closed on April 8, 1999?
- a.) Adventure Island
- b.) Discovery Island
- c.) Pleasure Island
- d.) River Country

61. Where was the *Legend of the Lion King* found?
- a.) Disney's Animal Kingdom
- b.) Fantasyland
- c.) The Studios
- d.) Frontierland

62. Which character is featured on the back of FASTPASS tickets?
- a.) Mickey
- b.) Minnie
- c.) Donald
- d.) Goofy

63. In what year did WDW's first water park open?
- a.) 1976
- b.) 1978
- c.) 1980
- d.) 1982

64. The Dimensional Duplicator is used in which WDW attraction?
- a.) *Stitch's Great Escape*
- b.) *DINOSAUR*
- c.) *Honey, I Shrunk the Audience*
- d.) *Journey Into Imagination with Figment*

65. Where did the white sands that make up the beach of the Seven Leas Lagoon come from?
- a.) The beaches of Tampa Bay
- b.) Reedy Creek
- c.) The "sands" are a man-made synthetic material.
- d.) Bay Lake

66. What Disneyland attraction was never intended to be built in WDW?
- a.) *Space Mountain*
- b.) *Pirates of the Caribbean*
- c.) *The Haunted Mansion*
- d.) *it's a small world*

67. Mermaid Tales Theater can be found in ___?
- a.) *Conservation Station*
- b.) The Studios' Animation Courtyard
- c.) Disney's Polynesian Resort
- d.) *Ariel's Grotto* in the MK

68. Where can you hear the Society Orchestra?
- a.) Main Street, U.S.A.
- b.) Beach Club Resort
- c.) *Twilight Zone Tower of Terror*
- d.) Grand Floridian Resort & Spa

Did You Know?

IT WAS WALT DISNEY HIMSELF WHO BROUGHT THE IDEA OF USING TOPIARIES (LIVING PLANTS TRAINED AND PRUNED INTO ORNAMENTAL SHAPES) TO HIS THEME PARKS.

69. Who oversaw the overall construction of Walt Disney World?
  a.) Michael Eisner's father, William Eisner
  b.) Admiral Joe Fowler
  c.) Roy O. Disney
  d.) General "Joe" Potter

70. What attraction floats on the Chakranadi River?
  a.) *Jungle Cruise*
  b.) *Kali River Rapids*
  c.) *Discovery Radio Cruise*
  d.) *Shrunken Ned's Junior Jungle Boats*

71. "Danger! The emergency destruct system is now activated. The ship will detonate in five minutes" can be heard in ___?
  a.) *Stitch's Great Escape*
  b.) *The Timekeeper*
  c.) *DINOSAUR*
  d.) *The Great Movie Ride*

72. Which of the following is NOT one of the islands located in the Seven Seas Lagoon?
  a.) Palm Isle
  b.) Beachcomber Isle
  c.) Castaway Cay
  d.) Blackbeard's Island

73. The Latin motto "Otium Cum Dignitate" appears where?
  a.) St. Mark's Square, in the Italy pavilion
  b.) Behind the front desk at the Grand Floridian
  c.) Port Orleans – Riverside
  d.) The Rose and Crown Pub in Epcot's United Kingdom

74. What was the former name of Walt Disney Imagineering?
  a.) WED Enterprises
  b.) MAPO
  c.) Walter Elias Disney
  d.) World Engineering Division

75. How many attractions did WDW offer when it opened on October 1, 1971?
  a.) 14
  b.) 19

c.) 23

d.) 29

76. Where could you take "A Journey Through Time and Space"?

a.) *The Timekeeper*

b.) *DINOSAUR*

c.) *Mission: SPACE*

d.) *Space Mountain*

77. What was one of Walt's requirements for his vision of EPCOT, the city?

a.) There would be no gas-powered cars.

b.) There would be no sales tax.

c.) Everyone must be employed.

d.) All residents over the age of 18 must graduate high school.

78. Phylicia Rashad, who plays Dr. Marsh in the *DINOSAUR* attraction, once appeared in ___?

a.) *Superstar Television*

b.) *Monster Sound Show*

c.) *Horizons*

d.) *Backstage Studio Tour*

79. Where were Cast Members sent for training prior to the opening of WDW in 1971?

a.) Disneyland

b.) Walt Disney Studios in Burbank, California

c.) The Celebrity Sports Center in Denver, Colorado

d.) Walt Disney's hometown in Missouri

80. Which of these feature films never had an attraction or parade at WDW?

a.) *Mulan*

b.) *Toy Story*

c.) *Ace Ventura: Pet Detective*

d.) *Treasure Planet*

81. "My nerves are shot. How do I get myself into these situations?" could be heard in ___?

a.) *Jim Henson's MuppetVision 3-D*

b.) *Voyage of the Little Mermaid*

c.) *Ellen's Energy Adventure*

d.) *It's Tough to be a Bug!*

82. What attraction did *Mission to Mars* replace?

Did You Know?

THERE ARE ENOUGH DISNEY CHARACTER T-SHIRTS SOLD IN WDW EACH YEAR TO PUT MICKEY MOUSE'S SMILING FACE ON THE CHEST OF EVERY PERSON IN CHICAGO.

a.) *Horizons*
b.) *If You Had Wings*
c.) *Flight to the Moon*
d.) *Star Jets*

83. Where can you sail "the River of Time"?
a.) *Liberty Square Riverboat*
b.) Mexico pavilion
c.) *Kali River Rapids*
d.) *Jungle Cruise*

84. In what order did the WDW theme parks open?
a.) Magic Kingdom (the MK), Epcot, Disney–MGM Studios (the Studios), Disney's Animal Kingdom (DAK)
b.) MK, DAK, Epcot, the Studios
c.) MK, the Studios, Epcot, DAK
d.) MK, Epcot, DAK, the Studios

85. Which of these "mountains" is the shortest?
a.) Big Thunder Mountain
b.) Mount Mayday
c.) Space Mountain
d.) Splash Mountain

86. The Trumbo Canal can be found where?
a.) Old Key West Resort
b.) Epcot's Italy pavilion
c.) Port Orleans – Riverside
d.) Fantasia Gardens Miniature Golf

87. What did Walt Disney not include in his "Florida Project"?

a.) A 100-acre industrial park
b.) An airport
c.) A convention center
d.) A second Disney movie studio

88. Where can you see a salute to all nations, but mostly America?
a.) *The American Adventure*
b.) *IllumiNations*
c.) *Jim Henson's MuppetVision 3-D*
d.) *The Hall of Presidents*

89. "That's what you think, you long drink of water!" can be heard in ___?
a.) *The Hall of Presidents*
b.) *Mickey's PhilharMagic*
c.) *Honey, I Shrunk the Audience*
d.) *It's Tough to be a Bug!*

90. What is the deepest body of water in WDW?
a.) Bay Lake
b.) Seven Seas Lagoon
c.) World Showcase Lagoon
d.) *The Living Seas* aquarium tank

91. "Walk Around The World" commemorative bricks were first offered in ___?
a.) 1971
b.) 1989
c.) 1994
d.) 1999

92. Where would you have found the Goofy Pose-a-Matic?

a.) Disney Village Marketplace
b.) *ImageWorks* at Epcot's Imagination! Pavilion
c.) Main Street, U.S.A.
d.) Disney-MGM Studios

93. At which of these locations will you NOT find a pyramid?
a.) Mexico pavilion
b.) Imagination! Pavilion
c.) Coronado Springs Resort
d.) *Kali River Rapids*

94. You can go rock climbing at ___?
a.) Blizzard Beach
b.) DisneyQuest
c.) Coronado Springs Resort
d.) Fort Wilderness Resort & Campground

95. What was the price of admission to the Magic Kingdom on Opening Day 1971?
a.) Free (yeah, right)
b.) $3.50 to $4.95
c.) $9.99
d.) $19.71

96. Which Circle-Vision 360 film

opened in May of 2003?
a.) *The Timekeeper*
b.) *Reflections of China*
c.) *O Canada!*
d.) *Magic Carpet 'Round the World*

97. Who was the first family to enter the Magic Kingdom on opening day?
a.) The Bill Windsor family
b.) The Disney family
c.) Richard Nixon and the First Family
d.) L.C. Valerie and family

98. Where could you enjoy the *Sorcery In The Sky* show?
a.) Magic Kingdom
b.) Epcot
c.) Disney-MGM Studios
d.) Disney's Animal Kingdom

99. What government body has final say over the building and maintenance of WDW's roads and buildings?
a.) Lake Buena Vista
b.) Reedy Creek Improvement District

Did You Know?

ON FEBRUARY 27, 1992, WDW CAST MEMBERS PLANTED MORE THAN 50,000 PINE TREES ACROSS 50 ACRES TO FORM A "HIDDEN MICKEY" IN HONOR OF WDW'S 20TH ANNIVERSARY.

c.) Downtown Disney Municipal Works

d.) WED Enterprises Orlando

100. "Nothing is rehearsed . . . We don't know what will happen, but . . . You'll be there" can be heard in ___?

a.) *Mission: SPACE*

b.) *Kilimanjaro Safaris*

c.) *Lights! Motors! Action! Stunt Show*

d.) *Sounds Dangerous*

101. Which attraction lets you choose your own ending?

a.) *Body Wars*

b.) *Mission: SPACE*

c.) *Star Tours*

d.) *Walt Disney World Railroad*

102. Where can you find "thrilling adventure through dark mysterious caverns"?

a.) *Maelstrom*

b.) *Tom Sawyer Island*

c.) *Pirates of the Caribbean*

d.) *It's Tough to be a Bug!*

103. What attraction is described as "It's Fast. It's a Blast. It's in the Past"?

a.) *Primeval Whirl*

b.) *DINOSAUR*

c.) *Hall of Presidents*

d.) *Rock 'n' Roller Coaster*

104. Guests can taste Coca-Cola flavors from around the world in what venue?

a.) Tomorrowland Café

b.) World Showcase

c.) Club Cool

d.) Downtown Disney

105. Where will you find the "Lights of Winter"?

a.) Magic Kingdom

b.) Downtown Disney

c.) Disney-MGM Studios

d.) Epcot

106. In what attraction can you hear the voice of Don Rickles?

a.) *The Enchanted Tiki Room – Under New Management*

b.) *Cranium Command*

c.) *The Timekeeper*

d.) *Journey Into Imagination with Figment*

107. Which restaurant does NOT offer Character Dining?

a.) Cape May Café

b.) Crystal Palace

c.) Whispering Canyon Café

d.) Akershus Royal Banquet Hall

108. What is WDW's tallest resort?
a.) Wilderness Lodge
b.) The WDW Dolphin
c.) Contemporary Resort
d.) Grand Floridian Resort & Spa

109. Where could you find the "Energy Exchange"?
a.) Universe of Energy pavilion
b.) *Tomorrowland Indy Speedway*
c.) CommuniCore East
d.) *Conservation Station*

110. What Disney TV show and movie inspired the now-defunct *Mike Fink Keelboats* attraction?
a.) *Wonderful World of Disney*
b.) *Davy Crockett and the River Pirates*
c.) *The Adventures of Mike Fink*
d.) None; it was developed specifically for the Magic Kingdom

111. "Warning! Remain in your vehicle. The area you are entering is extremely dangerous" can be heard in ___?
a.) *Test Track*
b.) *Mission: SPACE*
c.) *Expedition Everest*
d.) *The Great Movie Ride*

112. Where can you find "a beacon for the show business elite"?
a.) *Tower of Terror*
b.) Hollywood Brown Derby
c.) *The Great Movie Ride*
d.) All-Star Movies Resort

113. Who was hired by Walt Disney to act as a model when the Imagineers were creating the first Audio-Animatronics figures?
a.) Fred Astaire
b.) Buddy Ebsen
c.) Sammy Davis, Jr.
d.) Dean Martin

114. What was the "Millennium Village"?
a.) A Downtown Disney shop
b.) An area of Disney's Animal Kingdom
c.) The area that housed the foreign students working in World Showcase
d.) A World Showcase pavilion

115. On what attraction do you hear, "Ready when you are, C.B."?
a.) *The Great Movie Ride*
b.) *Sounds Dangerous*
c.) *The American Adventure*
d.) *Kilimanjaro Safaris*

116. Where could you hear, "So that's the Norwegian doing the hoochie-coochie . . ."?
a.) *Jim Henson's MuppetVision 3-D*
b.) *Sounds Dangerous*
c.) *Carousel of Progress*
d.) *Maelstrom*

117. An agreement with the city of Orlando and the state of Florida gives Disney the right to ___?
a.) Form its own labor union

b.) Construct a nuclear power plant

c.) Charge a toll for visitors exiting the highway

d.) Appoint a Disney executive as mayor of Orlando

118. What did Walt Disney propose as the main mode of transportation for his original vision of EPCOT, the city?

a.) Walking

b.) Bicycles

c.) Electric cars

d.) PeopleMovers

119. The motto of the Lake Buena Vista Fire Department is ___?

a.) The Pixie Dust Brigade

b.) Faith, Trust and Pixie Dust

c.) Protecting the Magic

d.) To Protect the Dreams

120. Who (or what) were Hooter, Fuzzball, the Geex, Major Domo, and Minor Domo?

a.) The names of ride cars in *Mr. Toad's Wild Ride*

b.) Adventurers Club characters

c.) *Cranium Command* characters

d.) Captain EO's crew

121. The attraction with the tallest height requirement in all of WDW can be found in ___?

a.) Magic Kingdom

b.) Epcot

c.) Disney-MGM Studios

d.) Disney's Animal Kingdom

122. Where is the "Home of the Victory Dog"?

a.) Toy Story Pizza Planet

b.) Tony's Town Square Restaurant

c.) Rosie's All American Café

d.) Mickey's Toontown Fair

123. What was billed as a "New Ride for the New Year"?

a.) *Test Track*

b.) *Journey Into Imagination*

c.) *Soarin'*

d.) *Expedition Everest*

124. Can you name the water ski show that was performed at WDW in the early 1970s?

a.) *Seven Skis Water Pageant*

b.) *The Wonderful World of Water Ski Show*

c.) *Disney Wide World of Water Show*

d.) *Disney FantaSea*

125. Where could you hear, "Trust me. What could go wrong?"

a.) *Star Tours*

b.) *DINOSAUR*

c.) *Jim Henson's MuppetVision 3-D*

d.) *Honey, I Shrunk the Audience*

126. You'd find *Amazon Annie, Irrawaddy Irma,* and *Wamba Wanda* in ___?

a.) *Kilimanjaro Safaris*

b.) Adventurers Club

c.) *Discovery River Taxis*

d.) *Jungle Cruise*

127. *The Magical World of Barbie* **stage show was performed in the ___?**

    a.) America Gardens Theatre in Epcot

    b.) Cinderella Castle Forecourt Stage

    c.) Fantasyland Theater

    d.) Galaxy Palace Theater in Tomorrowland

128. Where could you find "South Island"?

    a.) Crescent Lake

    b.) Disney's Polynesian Resort

    c.) Rivers of America

    d.) Seven Seas Lagoon

129. Which of these attractions was never sponsored by General Electric?

    a.) *IllumiNations*

    b.) *Journey Into Imagination*

    c.) *Carousel of Progress*

    d.) *Horizons*

130. What film starring Robin Williams and Walter Cronkite was once seen at WDW?

    a.) *Aladdin – Behind the Scenes with the Genie*

    b.) *One Man's Dream*

    c.) *Back to Neverland*

    d.) *Walt Disney's Animated Adventures*

131. The second "Official Airline of Walt Disney World" was ___?

Did You Know?

THE PGA TOUR'S FUNAI CLASSIC IS PLAYED ON DISNEY'S PALM AND MAGNOLIA GOLF COURSES.

a.) Delta Airlines
b.) United Airlines
c.) Eastern Airlines
d.) Continental Airlines

132. You can "Come in a Stranger, Leave a Little Stranger" in ___?
a.) *The Enchanted Tiki Room – Under New Management*
b.) *Adventurers Club*
c.) Pecos Bill Café
d.) *The Haunted Mansion*

133. The live nativity presentation at the Disney Village Marketplace was called ___?
a.) *The Glory and Pageantry of Christmas*
b.) *Disney's Holiday Magic*
c.) *Christmas in the Village*
d.) *Disney's Christmas Pageant*

134. What was built on WDW property but never implemented?
a.) A permanent residential community
b.) A multi-level parking garage
c.) A building for a ride based on the animated film, *Treasure Planet*
d.) A police station

135. "Get outta here, ya little numbskulls. I love ya. Thank you for coming . . . I think. GET OUT!" could be heard in ___?
a.) *The Enchanted Tiki Room*
b.) *The Timekeeper*

c.) *Festival of the Lion King*
d.) *Flights of Wonder*

136. You can find Ruthless Billy Jack in ___?
a.) *Kilimanjaro Safaris*
b.) *Kali River Rapids*
c.) *Frontierland Shootin' Arcade*
d.) *The Great Movie Ride*

137. The first Circle-Vision 360 movie to be shown at WDW was ___?
a.) *America the Beautiful*
b.) *O Canada!*
c.) *Magic Carpet 'Round the World*
d.) *American Journeys*

138. You'll find "good books – the recordings of man's ideas and achievements" in ___?
a.) *Spaceship Earth*
b.) Exposition Hall on Main Street, U.S.A.
c.) *Swiss Family Treehouse*
d.) Sid Cahuenga's One of a Kind Shop

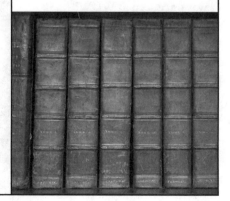

THE ANSWERS
TO CHAPTER ONE

1. a) Inside Cinderella Castle
Space for an apartment for the Disney family was created high inside Cinderella Castle. However, Walt passed away before the Magic Kingdom and the apartment were completed, and the apartment was left unfinished. Over the years, the space (which is serviced by an elevator) has been used for storage, a telephone switchboard, and a Cast Member dressing room. Want to see where the apartment is? Look for three tall windows with pointed arches near the top of the Castle, facing Fantasyland and Liberty Square.

2. b.) Disney's Wild Animal Kingdom
Michael Eisner and Disney Imagineers announced Disney's Wild Animal Kingdom project on June 5, 1995. Groundbreaking followed just two months later. The name was changed to "Disney's Animal Kingdom" before the park's Grand Opening on April 22, 1998.

3. c.) October 29, 1971
WDW opened on October 1, 1971, but to avoid the problems encountered when Disneyland opened, such as bathrooms and water fountains that didn't work, Disney postponed the official dedication and press events for WDW for a few weeks to ensure that everything would function smoothly. The event was taped and broadcast "in living color" on NBC on October 29, 1971, in a 90-minute TV special called *The Grand Opening of Walt Disney World*.

4. c.) Disney's Animal Kingdom
Disney Imagineers have created a total of 18 "mountains" worldwide in the Disney theme parks. At 199 feet tall, the *Expedition Everest* mountain

in DAK is not only WDW's tallest but its newest. In fact, it is the tallest "mountain" in the state of Florida.

5. a.) *Big Thunder Mountain Railroad*

Cousin Elrod is the "washed-up" miner floating in his long-johns in the bathtub during the flash flood scene.

6. d.) Disney's Magical Express

As part of the 2005-2006 "Happiest Celebration on Earth," honoring Disneyland's 50th Anniversary, WDW announced an innovative new service called "Disney's Magical Express." It offered Disney Resort Guests complimentary airport shuttle service, luggage delivery to the Guest's resort room, and airline check-in for the return flight.

7. b.) 43 miles

When Walt Disney purchased the 47 square miles that were to become WDW as we know it today, the property was nothing more than desolate swampland, scrub forests, and groves. Massive amounts of earth had to be moved to transform this area into what's become the world's number one vacation destination. Since much of central Florida is, in essence, a thin layer of land "floating" on a body of water, Disney faced a daunting ecological challenge. It had to transform the area without damaging the water supply because if

any part of it were damaged or destroyed, it would have caused a massive ecological imbalance that would have affected the entire region. To ensure the area's environmental health, Disney set aside a 7,500-acre Conservation Area in 1970 and developed a system of more than 43 miles of canals and 22 miles of levees that blend into the natural landscape and control the water levels automatically.

8. a.) *The Enchanted Tiki Room – Under New Management*

Near the end of the show, Iago tells everyone to stand up. Michael then says, "as long as you're all standing …" and José continues, "We have a wonderful magic trick for you." Don't know what the trick is? Easy — they make the whole audience disappear!

9. b.) Leased the entire Disney Inn Resort

On February 1, 1994, the Department of Defense (DOD) leased the Disney Inn Resort for exclusive use by retired and active military personnel and their families, members of the reserves and the National Guard, and DOD civilians. These personnel were entitled to special hotel rates, substantially discounted attraction tickets, on-site laundry facilities, and tax-free Disney merchandise. The DOD subsequently purchased the hotel outright and changed its name to "Shades of Green" to signify the camouflage uniforms worn by the armed forces.

10. d.) Explosives

Next to the U.S. military, Walt Disney World is the largest purchaser of explosives in the United States. Explosives? Yes; remember, there are fireworks shows in two parks every night of the week, 365 days a year, as well as countless pyrotechnics used in shows and attractions throughout the resorts. Downtown Disney used to have a nightly fireworks show, too, to celebrate "New Year's Eve." The last one was December 31, 2005, fittingly a real New Year's Eve celebration.

11. d.) Minnie

On May 5, 1987, Disney issued "Disney Dollars," its own special currency, good for purchases at Disney parks and retail stores. Mickey's face was featured on the $1 bill, with Goofy gracing a $5. Disney issued a $10 bill featuring Minnie on November 20, 1989. The idea for a Disney Dollars currency came about when Disney was preparing for the opening of the first Disney Store (on March 27, 1987) in the Glendale Galleria in California. The currency was invented as a new form of gift certificate. New bills are now issued regularly and are becoming quite collectible.

12. c.) *Jim Henson's Muppet Vision 3-D*

This "warning" can be heard at the beginning of the show.

13. a.) Fantasyland

Walt Disney once said of Fantasyland: "Here is the world of imagination, hopes and dreams. In this timeless land of enchantment, the age of chivalry, magic and make believe are reborn and fairy tales come true. Fantasyland is dedicated to the young at heart — to those who believe that when you wish upon a star, your dreams come true."

14. b.) *Lights, Motors, Action!*

During the gala that began May 5, 2005, Disney parks around the

world celebrated the 50th anniversary of the opening of Disneyland with the 18-month "Happiest Celebration on Earth." Three of WDW's four theme parks received a "gift" from the other Disney properties. The Studios received *Lights, Motors, Action! Extreme Stunt Show* from Paris, Epcot received *Soarin'* from California, and the MK got *Cinderellabration* from Tokyo.

15. d.) *Pirates of the Caribbean*
The Torre del Cielo ("Sky Tower") stands near the entrance to *Pirates of the Caribbean* on Caribbean Plaza in the MK. Near the top of this tall tower, you will find a working clock.

16. b.) A Florida state senator
In October 1964, Florida state senator Irlo Bronson sold the first large parcel of land that ultimately became the WDW property. He sold his 8,380 acres of desolate swampland for a whopping $107 per acre. The sale was the first of literally hundreds of real estate transactions that would ultimately add up to 27,258 acres.

17. c.) *Tomorrowland Transit Authority*
As your Metroliner hugs the exterior walls of *Space Mountain*, a woman's voice makes this humorous announcement.

18. a.) *Fantasmic!*
Fantasmic! premiered in Disneyland in 1992 and opened at WDW's Disney-MGM Studios in October 1998. This multimedia production is offered nightly in the Hollywood Hills Amphitheater, which holds more than 9,000 Guests.

19. d.) Jimmy Stewart
The NBC broadcast of WDW's opening featured a number of celebrities, among them country music star Glen Campbell (who performed songs throughout the show), Julie Andrews, comedian Jonathan Winters, Los Angeles Lakers' sportscaster Chick Hern, auto racing legends Bobby Unser and Jackie Stewart, and funny-man "Buddy" Hackett. Bob Hope recounted Walt Disney's legacy as the show drew to its conclusion: a parade down Main Street, U.S.A. starring Disney characters and 1,076 musicians under the direction of *Music Man* composer Meredith Wilson.

20. a.) Contemporary Resort
The Contemporary's Olympiad Health Club and Spa has exercise equipment, a sauna, tanning booths, and massages by appointment.

21. d.) 70,000
Bay Lake, located near Disney's Contemporary and Wilderness Lodge Resorts, was stocked with 70,000 fish when WDW first opened. Why? Well, you can charter a captained boat and go on a catch-

and-release fishing excursion from both resorts. The largest largemouth bass ever caught was a whopping 14.25 pounds. (Really.)

22. b.) Jiminy Cricket
Disney's expanding responsibility in protecting natural resources led to the creation of a new corporate office of Environmental Affairs in 1990. Jiminy Cricket serves as the official "conscience" for Disney's "Environmentality" programs, promoting preservation.

23. c.) *The Living Seas*
Opened in 1986, *The Living Seas* was the first WDW attraction to incorporate live animals into the actual attraction. Its 203-foot diameter tank is home to more than 8,500 inhabitants, representing over 100 different species of marine life.

24. c.) 20,000
In a 1966 promotional film, Uncle Walt outlined his dream for a futuristic, planned community that would showcase American industry and research, provide the finest of cultural and educational opportunities, and be home to 20,000 permanent residents. He envisioned it as a place to explore new ideas in urban planning, including encasing the entire city with a dome.

25. c.) 1999
The FASTPASS system was first deployed in WDW at its newest theme park, Disney's Animal Kingdom, following testing in both the Florida and Anaheim resorts. It gained popularity fast. On February 17, 2003, WDW celebrated the distribution of its 100 millionth FASTPASS ticket. Mary Dillon of Atlanta, Georgia, was visiting the Studios with her husband and their three children when she received the FASTPASS for the *Rock 'n' Roller Coaster*. As her ticket slid out of the machine, she was startled by music and silver streamers. WDW President Al Weiss then surprised her with a Golden FASTPASS that provided her and her family FASTPASS entry to all 23 attractions offering FASTPASS in the four WDW theme parks. The whole family also received com-

Did You Know?

EACH YEAR, ENOUGH KETCHUP PACKETS ARE HANDED OUT THAT, IF LAID END TO END, THEY WOULD STRETCH FROM THE MAGIC KINGDOM TO MINNEAPOLIS, MINNESOTA!

memorative jackets and a personal tour from a Disney Tour Guide.

26. b.) *DINOSAUR*
You hear this instruction from Dr. Seeker during the pre-show movie.

27. a.) Disney-MGM Studios
Once Upon a Time is a shop on Sunset Boulevard in the Studios. It is housed in a replica of the famous Spanish-style Carthay Circle Theater, which opened in Hollywood in 1926 on Wilshire Boulevard. Sadly, it was demolished on March 18, 1969, to make way for a shopping mall. The theater is honored in WDW because *Snow White and the Seven Dwarfs* premiered there in 1937, with Walt in attendance.

28. b.) The Orange Bird
Housed in the Sunshine Pavilion, a three million-dollar, pagoda-style building, *The Enchanted Tiki Birds Starring in the Tropical Serenade* was one of the MK's opening day attractions. The sponsor, Florida Citrus Growers, had Disney create the Orange Bird as a mascot for the pavilion. (Creative, huh?) Up until 1986, the Orange Bird, in his bright orange bird suit with yellow breast and giant orange for a head, could be seen walking around Adventureland — especially near the Sunshine Tree Terrace, a place to get (what else?) orange juice and other citrus drinks. When the Citrus Growers'

sponsorship expired that year, the Orange Bird flew the coop as well.

29. c.) Port Orleans Resort – French Quarter
Doubloon Lagoon is one of the most popular themed pools in all of WDW. It includes a fantastic Mardi Gras dragon slide and alligator fountains.

30. d.) To complete construction of one of the resorts
When Allen Contracting, the general contractor responsible for the construction of Disney's first hotels, said in 1970 that there was no way they could finish in time for a October 1971 opening, Admiral Joe Fowler fired them. He felt that if they couldn't do it, Disney could, and the Buena Vista Construction Company was formed. It hired many of the same subcontractors (and many Allen employees) and finished the job on time.

31. b.) A pneumatic trash collection system
WDW was the first to install the Swedish-built Automated Vacuum Assisted Collection (AVAC) in the U.S. Its pneumatic tubes are located beneath the surface of the Magic Kingdom, on the Utilidors' 15-foot ceilings. The tubes connect to trash collection points throughout the park (one notable exception being Tom Sawyer Island). Waste from

the park's trash cans is dropped into the collection points and pushed at speeds of up to 60 mph to a central compactor station (located behind *Splash Mountain*) every 15 minutes by blasts of compressed air. If the system were ever to clog, simply dropping a rock into one of the tubes would clear out the blockage. (The second, and only other, AVAC system in the U.S. can be found on New York City's Roosevelt Island.)

32. a.) Rafiki's Planet Watch
Above the entrance to the station in Africa in Disney's Animal Kingdom, you'll find the invitation to "Open Your Eyes to the World Around You" when you take the *Wildlife Express Train* to Rafiki's Planet Watch. By doing so, you'll not only see what others are doing to save the environment and endangered animals, but learn what you can do as well.

33. b.) An Epcot show about computers
Backstage Magic replaced the outdated *Astuter Computer Revue* in CommuniCore East in February 1984, making the latter the first attraction to be removed from Epcot. The new show focused on the history of computers and explained how they were used at WDW. It ran for nearly 10 years before closing in 1993.

34. c.) 2

There are two Circle-Vision films shown in the WDW theme parks as we go to press, both in Epcot's World Showcase. They are *Reflections of China* in the China pavilion and *O Canada!* in Canada. Circle-Vision films are unique: they are projected onto nine screens that line the perimeter of the theater for a full 360-degree experience. You stand to view them, so the theaters that show them have no seats.

35. b.) *Star Tours*
Star Tours is sponsored by Energizer — the battery that is "long-lasting." Get it?

36. a.) *Pirates of the Caribbean*
Right after your boat travels over the falls, you are warned by an old pirate's voice, "you may not survive to pass this way again . . . Dead men tell no tales."

37. d.) *Country Bear Jamboree*
Ursus R. Bear was the founder of Grizzly Hall, the building that houses the *Country Bear Jamboree*. His name, dates (1848-1928), and

picture can be found above the attraction's main stage.

38. c.) The Earth Globe used in _IllumiNations: Reflections of Earth_

Earth Globe, the centerpiece of _IllumiNations_, is the world's first spherical video display system. The Globe is 28 feet in diameter, stands more than three stories tall, and is covered with more than 15,000 Light-Emitting Diodes in the shape of the continents. It rotates on a 350-ton floating island that houses six computer processors, 258 strobe lights, and an infrared guidance system. In the show's finale, the Globe opens and a flaming torch rises from its center 40 feet into the air.

39. d.) _Big Thunder Mountain Railroad_

"Dave V. Jones Mine" is one of the scenes along the _BTMRR_. Look for it right after the "Flash Flood" scene and just before the "Winch House."

40. d.) Roy E. Disney

Roy's name can be found on a window on the second story of Main Street, U.S.A. It reads, in part:
Roy E. Disney
Specializing in the Gentlemanly Sport of Racing at Sea Aboard the Ketch Peregrina
Sailmaker – Sailing Lessons
Roy Edward Disney, who is listed with his wife, Patty, and their four children, is Walt's nephew, the son of Walt's brother, Roy Oliver Disney. Nephew Roy is a sailing enthusiast, with a trophy named in his honor at the Pacific Coast Interscholastic Sailing Association.

41. c.) _Twilight Zone Tower of Terror_

The Studios' *Star Tours*, based on the *Star Wars* saga created by George Lucas, isn't the only Lucas/Disney collaboration you'll find in WDW. It is actually the sixth theme-park collaboration between Lucas and The Walt Disney Company. The others are *Captain EO* and *The ExtraTERRORestrial Alien Encounter* (both now retired), the Studios' *Indiana Jones Epic Stunt Spectacular*, Disneyland's *Indiana Jones Adventure*, and the Disneyland Paris *Indiana Jones et le Temple du Peril*.

42. a.) A former performance group

A group of performers in the Italy pavilion in World Showcase (who also once appeared in France), the members of Imaginum were costumed to look like white stone statues come to life. They may have looked like statutes, but they were never taken for "granite."

43. d.) *Jungle Cruise*

Schweitzer Falls is the name of a waterfall in the *Jungle Cruise* which, according to your Skipper, was named after the famous "Dr. Albert . . . Falls."

44. a.) *The American Adventure*

This line is an excerpt from the Apollo 11 moon landing of July 20, 1969. The landing, which was " . . . one small step for a man, one giant leap for mankind . . ." was seen on TV by hundreds of millions of people around the globe. The transcript of the landing dialogue is:
Lunar module pilot Edwin E. "Buzz" Aldrin, Jr.:
"Thirty feet, two and a half, down. Faint shadow . . . Four forward. Four forward. Drifting to the right a little. Okay. Down a half . . ."
Capsule Communicator Charles Duke:
"We copy you down, Eagle . . ."
Commander Neil A. Armstrong:
"Tranquility Base here. The Eagle has landed."
Capsule Communicator Duke:
"Roger, Tranquility. We copy you on the ground. You got a bunch of guys about to turn blue. We're breathing again. Thanks a lot."

45. c.) *Great Moments at the Movies*

According to early design concepts for the Disney-MGM Studios theme park (including preview guides and early maps), *The Great Movie Ride* was originally going to be called "Great Moments at the Movies" and was to be sponsored by Sears. Instead of an attraction featuring classic movie scenes starring Audio-Animatronics figures, it was going to have live celebrity impersonators portraying all of the characters! However, the Sears sponsorship never came through, and the ride's name and concept changed prior to the park's opening in 1989.

46. a.) *Honey, I Shrunk the Audience*
As you enter the queue area of this attraction, you enter the fictitious "Imagination Institute." Here, you will see signs referring to the presentation of the "Inventor of the Year Award" (which is "Presented Through a Generous Grant from Kodak") to Professor Wayne Szalinski, who will demonstrate his incredible shrinking machine.

47. a.) *Country Bear Jamboree*
Introduced as the Sunbonnets from the Sunshine State (that's Florida to you and me), Bunny, Bubbles, and Beulah sing their hit, "All the Guys that Turn Me On Turn Me Down." Bunny, Bubbles, and Beulah were voiced by Loulie Jean Norman, Peggy Clark, and Jackie Ward, respectively.

48. b.) *Pirates of the Caribbean*
The fort that houses the *Pirates of the Caribbean* attraction was modeled after San Juan's famous fortress, the Castillo del Morro ("morro" means promontory, and the citadel's full name is el Castillo de San Felipe del Morro). The six-level fortress was built with 20-foot thick, 140-foot high walls to protect the city from attacks by sea during the 17th and 18th centuries. It also served as a gateway to "New Spain."

49. a.) *Let's Make a Deal*
In the spring of 1990, the classic TV game show, *Let's Make a Deal*, was brought to the Studios. It consisted of a show that was televised daily on NBC, as well as a second show used to promote the Studios (which had opened less than a year earlier). Although it didn't have the legendary Monty Hall as host when the show opened (he returned to the show later that year), it did have one of the show's primary elements — a fully costumed audience ready to take a chance on door number one . . . or what was in the box.

50. b.) Jack Nicklaus
In 1971, Jack Nicklaus won the first "Walt Disney World Open Invitational." Oh, yeah . . . he won it the next two years as well! In 1974, the tournament switched to a team format and was called the "Walt Disney World National Team Championship." It didn't switch back to individual play until 1982. The name has changed several times over the years, to the "Walt Disney World Golf Classic" (1982), the "Walt Disney World/Oldsmobile Classic" (1985), the "National Car Rental Golf Classic at Walt Disney World" (1998), the "Disney Golf Classic" (2002), and "FUNAI Classic at the Walt Disney World Resort" (2003).

51. c.) Sundial
In 1987, Disney decided to consolidate WDW's back-office operations (then performed in a number

of leased spaces in Orlando) into a single new building to be constructed on property. Chairman of the Board Michael Eisner chose renowned Japanese architect Arata Isozaki to design the structure (now known as the Team Disney building) using "entertainment architecture." One of the elements Isozaki included is a huge sundial, a bow to the "Sunshine State" (Florida) in which it is located. The builders consulted with the Florida Solar Energy Center on the technical aspects to be sure it would actually work. The sundial is located inside the building's rotunda.

52. b.) *Carousel of Progress*
In the last scene, Father is cooking the holiday turkey. The modern oven starts beeping and the turkey starts to smoke. Then the oven door automatically slams open to reveal a burnt bird, announcing, "Bake mode complete. Enjoy your meal."

53. c.) Disney's Wilderness Lodge

Located in the Villas, The Iron Spike Room is a sitting room that displays extensive railroad memorabilia, such as photographs, rare plans and sketches, equipment, models, and more. A wonderful exhibit, on loan from the Disney family, includes rare photographs of Uncle Walt and the 1/8-scale Carolwood Pacific Railroad he had built in his backyard. Included are photos of two of the original Carolwood cars, which Roger Broggie built for Walt in the Disney Studios' machine shop.

54. d.) *Universe of Energy*
Cast Members guide you on a number of WDW rides. In Epcot's *Living with the Land* attraction, a CM takes you through greenhouses, biomes, and working laboratories to explain how man lives in harmony with the land and the environment. In *The Great Movie Ride*, a Cast Member takes you on a tour of the movies — and even gets involved in the action! The CMs on the *Jungle*

Did You Know?

WALT DISNEY WORLD IS ABOUT **80** TIMES THE SIZE OF THE ENTIRE COUNTRY OF MONACO.

Cruise are legendary not only for their ability to navigate the dangerous waterways, but also for their corny jokes!

55. b.) The 911 phone system

When Walt Disney and his Imagineers were designing his new theme park for Florida in the late 1960s, part of his dream included using the most advanced technologies available. This vision included a state-of-the-art telecommunications system. Disney decided that the best way to do it right was to do it themselves, and so, in 1969, they created their own independent telephone company in partnership with United Telephone Company of Florida. Called Vista-United Telecommunications, the company was co-owned by Vista Communications, Inc., a wholly owned Disney subsidiary that was created at the formation of the partnership. Vista-United has pioneered numerous firsts in the communications industry. In 1971, for example, it became the first fully electronic phone company, the first to use the 911 Emergency System in the state of Florida, and the first phone company to use only buried cable throughout its system.

56. a.) *Jim Henson's Muppet-Vision 3-D*

Right before the show's Grand Finale, Kermit asks Sam the Eagle if he's ready. Sam states that he's prepared "a glorious three-hour finale," to which Kermit replies, "You got a minute and a half."

57. c.) The Zanzibar Trading Co.

Located near the *Magic Carpets of Aladdin* ride in Adventureland, Zanzibar Trading is reminiscent of an open-air, Middle Eastern marketplace. The shop is filled with colorful clothing, spices, brassware, and other exotic souvenirs.

58. b.) *Body Wars*

Body Wars, located in the Wonders of Life pavilion in Epcot's Future World, took you on a "routine" medical mission where your probe was shrunk down to microscopic size and you were placed inside a person's body to rescue a colleague. The probe's Captain Jack Braddock was played by actor Tim Matheson, best known for his role as Eric "Otter" Stratton in the 1978 blockbuster film, *Animal House*. Who can forget the classic line: "TOGA! TOGA! TOGA!"

59. a.) *The American Adventure*

At the beginning of *The American Adventure*, Benjamin Franklin tells Mark Twain that pride is one of our national passions, and even those who overcome it are proud of their humility. Twain replies that he was born modest, but "fortunately, it wore off." He apparently said this

Did You Know?

THE WORLD-FAMOUS TURKEY LEGS SOLD THROUGHOUT WDW COME FROM 40- TO 50-POUND TURKEYS. EVERY 1.5-POUND LEG IS INJECTED WITH A SALT WATER CURE AND COOKED FOR 6 HOURS.

originally in an address to the YMCA at the Majestic Theatre in New York City, March 4, 1906. Another Twain line: "I am only human, although I regret it."

60. b.) Discovery Island
Located in Bay Lake (and called "Treasure Island" when it first opened to the public on April 8, 1974, as a bird sanctuary), 11.8-acre Discovery Island later became a nature park. It never caught on with the public, and when Disney's Animal Kingdom opened in 1998, it apparently sounded the death knell for the unpopular isle. Bay Lake's Discovery Island closed April 8, 1999, but its name lives on. In DAK, Discovery Island is the land that contains the *Tree of Life*.

61. b.) Fantasyland
Legend of the Lion King was a Fantasyland attraction in the Magic Kingdom. It opened on July 8, 1994, and closed on February 23,

2002. You'll find a similarly named attraction, *Festival of the Lion King*, in DAK's Camp Minnie-Mickey.

62. c.) Donald
Disney's free FASTPASS program, which allows Guests to cut down on wait times for popular park attractions, uses a ticketing system. You will find Donald Duck on the back of your ticket.

63. a.) 1976
WDW's first water park, River Country, opened June 20, 1976, next to the Fort Wilderness Resort on the shores of Bay Lake. Designed to resemble an old swimmin' hole, River Country looked like something right out of *Tom Sawyer* or *Huckleberry Finn,* with a secluded cove ("Bay Cove") and lush, grassy grounds. Its two "white-water rapids" inner-tube rides, huge heated swimming pool, two water slides, and rope swing offered activities

for the whole family. Guests could dine on fast food from Pop's Place and, during the busy season, at the Watering Hole. During the summer, River Country was the setting for an "All American Water Party," which included games and prizes for kids and adults and live bluegrass bands that played throughout the day. River Country was open seasonally from May through September through the fall of 2001. It did not reopen in 2002 and appears to have joined the ranks of WDW's bygone attractions.

64. c.) *Honey, I Shrunk the Audience*

Dr. Channing explains that the Dimensional Duplicator was developed "right here at the Imagination Institute" by Professor Szalinski and tells you that it can make exact replicas of any object at all.

65. d.) Bay Lake

Thirty years ago, there was no Seven Seas Lagoon. There was just a large, muddy marsh next to Bay Lake, the only natural body of water on the property. In fact, 450-acre Bay Lake and the land around it was one of the first pieces of property that Walt wanted to buy after flying over the region. (He was especially drawn to the large island in the lake's center, which later became Discovery Island.) The area to the west of the lake had a lot of high ground suit-

able for building, while the low land between it and the lake was mostly low wetlands that could not be built upon. Disney Imagineers decided to excavate part of the wetland and turn it into a man-made lagoon, which would provide additional space for swimming, boating, and other water sports, as well as a perfect setting for the planned Polynesian Village Resort. To accomplish this monumental feat, they dredged the wetlands adjacent to Bay Lake and then pumped the lake entirely dry and dredged out more than seven million cubic yards of muck and debris from the bottom. (The dirt was used to raise the site of the future Magic Kingdom by about 14 feet.) To the surprise of Disney engineers, the bottom of Bay Lake revealed thousands of tons of white sand. They cleaned it and used it to line the four and a half miles of beach around their new lagoon. Bay Lake and the new lagoon were refilled with water from the adjoining wetlands, and then connected by means of a "water bridge" and stocked with more than 70,000 bass. The Seven Seas Lagoon covers over 200 acres, contains three islands, and averages about 10 feet deep.

66. b.) *Pirates of the Caribbean*

Because Walt Disney felt Florida was so close to the Caribbean that people would not be interested in pirate lore, *Pirates of the Carib-*

Did You Know?

WHEN WDW TURNED 15 IN 1986, IT GAVE OUT
PRIZES EVERY 15 SECONDS. WINNERS TOOK HOME
EVERYTHING FROM SMALL BUTTONS TO
FULL-SIZED AUTOMOBILES!

bean was not originally planned for WDW. The Imagineers believed that an attraction with a theme that was less familiar to residents of the Southeast would be more appealing. Thus, the idea for Thunder Mesa with a *Western River Expedition* ride was developed. Plans for the ride were delayed, however, and after the park opened, repeated Guest inquiries about the location of the missing attraction that they'd loved so much at Disneyland prompted its construction in Adventureland.

67. a.) *Conservation Station*
In DAK's Mermaid Tales Theater, Shelley (get it? "Shell"-ee) the mermaid tells some great stories about kids' involvement in conservation around the world and how you can help save endangered species.

68. d.) **Grand Floridian Resort & Spa**
The four-story atrium in the lobby of Disney's flagship resort is often filled with the sounds of a grand piano and the Grand Floridian Society Orchestra. The jazz orchestra plays a variety of tunes, including themes from classic animated Disney films.

69. b.) **Admiral Joe Fowler**
Joseph Fowler was born on July 9, 1894. He graduated second in his class at the U.S. Naval Academy and later received a Master's Degree from M.I.T. A veteran of both World Wars, Rear Admiral Joe Fowler retired from the Navy in 1948 and began working for Walt Disney Productions in 1954. He was hired to oversee the construction of Disneyland and became its operations manager after it opened. In the late 1960s, Fowler was given the task of overseeing the construction of WDW. He later became a Senior Vice President of Walt Disney Productions, Chairman of the Board of WED, and Director of Buena Vista Construction Company. He retired from Disney in 1978 and passed away in 1993 at age 99.

70. b.) *Kali River Rapids*
The *Kali River Rapids* is a white-

water rafting adventure down the Chakranadi River in the Asia section of Disney's Animal Kingdom. Chakranadi River means "river that flows in a circle" in Thai.

71. d.) *The Great Movie Ride*
You hear this line in the *Alien* portion of the ride. It is spoken by Mother (the name of the ship's computer) when the self-destruct countdown begins.

72. a.) Palm Isle
When the Seven Seas Lagoon was created prior to the opening of WDW in 1971, Disney created three islands in it. Beachcomber Isle is located near the shores of the Polynesian Resort; Castaway Cay near the Grand Floridian, and Blackbeard's Island near the Contemporary (by the water bridge that connects the lagoon to Bay Lake). The three islands aren't open to Guests, but speakers hidden in their trees broadcast music to the shores of the Magic Kingdom resorts, and the islands also serve as launching areas for fireworks.

73. d.) The Rose and Crown Pub in Epcot's United Kingdom
"Leisure with Dignity" is the motto of the Rose and Crown Pub in the UK pavilion in World Showcase. Modeled after traditional pubs found throughout merry old England, it provides authentic British

dining options, including cottage pie and fish and chips. Grab a Guinness and join a jolly sing-a-long in the bar before or after your meal. (Or just skip the meal altogether and head straight for the Bass Ale!)

74. a.) WED Enterprises
In 1953, Walt Disney created a company that was separate from the Disney Studios to take over the design and construction of attractions for Disneyland, so as not to put any additional financial burden on the parent company. WED Enterprises, as he called it ("WED" for "Walter Elias Disney"), was later renamed "Walt Disney Imagineering" (WDI). Under that name, it continues to create, renovate, and expand all of the Walt Disney Company's theme parks. MAPO (short for Mary Poppins) is Disney's Manufacturing and Production division.

75. c.) 23
On WDW's opening day, the Magic Kingdom offered guests 23 attrac-

tions in six themed lands — four in Main Street, U.S.A., eight in Fantasyland, three in Adventureland, five in Frontierland, two in Liberty Square, and one in Tomorrowland. (Tomorrowland had a second attraction, the *Skyway*, which connected Tomorrowland and Fantasyland. But since there was just one *Skyway*, Disney counted it only once in its grand total and included it among the Fantasyland attractions.)

76. d.) *Space Mountain*

As you enter the *Space Mountain* building while riding the *Tomorrowland Transit Authority*, you will pass a sign that reads, "Space Mountain: A Journey Through Time and Space."

77. c.) Everyone must be employed.

In a 24-minute film recorded just before his death in 1966, Walt Disney presented to the media and government officials plans for his "Florida Project." In it he said, "In EPCOT there will be no slum areas because we won't let them develop. There will be no landowners and therefore no voting control. People will rent houses instead of buying them, and at modest rentals. There will be no retirees; everyone must be employed."

78. d.) *Backstage Studio Tour*

Phylicia Rashad's first appearance in a WDW attraction was in the original *Backstage Studio Tour* in the Studios. She and other cast members from the *Cosby Show* were featured in Soundstage 2 during the walking portion of the tour.

79. c.) The Celebrity Sports Center in Denver, Colorado

Owned by Walt Disney and a group of celebrity investors (including Art Linkletter), the center was used for training many of WDW's future Cast Members. The property was later purchased by Walt Disney Productions, which sold it in 1979. The complex was demolished in 1995.

80. d.) *Treasure Planet*

Ace Ventura Pet Detective: Live in Action parade began at the Studios in late 1995, but Ace's search for the albino bat didn't last very long. The *Toy Story* and *Mulan* parades were also seen in the Studios. The *Toy Story* parade ran throughout 1996 and was often matched with "Toy Story Weekends," during which Guests could meet some of their favorite characters from the film at the Pizza Planet Restaurant. The *Mulan* parade began on June 18, 1998, and ended its run in 2001.

81. b.) *Voyage of the Little Mermaid*

When Sebastian tells King Triton that "Somebody's got to nail dat girl's fins to de floor," the King agrees and tells him that he is just the crab to do it, to which Sebastian

Did You Know?

AS PART OF DISNEY'S COMMITMENT TO THE ENVIRONMENT AND THE LOCAL COMMUNITY, IT DONATES USED AND EXCESS BUILDING MATERIALS TO THE ORANGE COUNTY DISTRIBUTION CENTER, WHICH DISTRIBUTES THEM TO LOCAL NON-PROFIT ORGANIZATIONS.

replies, "Jumpin' jellyfish! My nerves are shot. How do I get myself into these situations?"

82. c.) *Flight to the Moon*

On Christmas Eve, 1971, *Flight to the Moon*, sponsored by McDonnell-Douglas, opened in Tomorrowland. Ironically, an attraction that was supposed to be taking place "sometime in the future" revolved around a feat that had been accomplished just a few years earlier — a space flight to the moon. After the pre-show to this D-ticket attraction, the 162 guests entered the circular theater and "Flight #92" took them to the moon. *Flight to the Moon* was replaced on June 7, 1975, by *Mission to Mars*, developed in conjunction

with NASA. The pre-show, and in fact much of the ride, was similar to its predecessor, although the host's name changed and a few women were now seen in the control room. When Guests entered the theater, they felt simulated G-forces as their shuttle lifted off for the red planet. Thanks to screens located on the floor and ceiling, they also saw the views from above and below as they approached the planet. *Mission to Mars* closed on October 4, 1993. It was eventually replaced by *The ExtraTERRORestrial Alien Encounter*.

83. b.) Mexico pavilion

The name of Mexico's ride in World Showcase is *El Rio del Tiempo*, which means, of course, "the river of time."

84. a.) Magic Kingdom, Epcot, Disney–MGM Studios, Disney's Animal Kingdom

WDW opened October 1, 1971, with the Magic Kingdom as its centerpiece and original theme park. Epcot opened exactly 11 years later, on October 1, 1982. The Studios' grand opening was May 1, 1989, followed by DAK's, April 22, 1998.

85. d.) Splash Mountain

At 87 feet high, Splash Mountain is the shortest of the five "major" mountains in WDW. Big Thunder Mountain stands 197 feet high, while Space Mountain and Mount Mayday stand 180 and 95 feet high, respectively. You'll find the first three in the MK and the last in Typhoon Lagoon.

86. a.) Old Key West Resort

The Trumbo Canal is Old Key West's "intercoastal waterway," which flows into the Sassagoula River. The waterway winds through the resort's "Keys," which feature a working lighthouse and a wooden pier reminiscent of the famous Mallory Pier in Key West, Florida. The Trumbo Ferry, a pontoon boat, transports Guests to the Port Orleans resorts and Downtown Disney.

87. d.) A second Disney movie studio

While some of Walt's original concepts for WDW survived his passing in one form or another, many did not. This is especially true of what Walt called EPCOT. His "Master Plan" for it called for a glass-domed city that would be home to a working community, an industrial complex, a 30-story hotel, an airport, and a conference center.

88. c.) *Jim Henson's Muppet-Vision 3-D*

Presented by Sam the Eagle, *MuppetVision*'s finale is a patriotic tribute — complete with toy soldiers, marching band, and of course, a few unscheduled surprises!

89. a.) *The Hall of Presidents*

When Abraham Lincoln says that he believes a government cannot endure permanently half-slave and half-free, a spectator calls out, "That's what you think, you long drink of water!"

90. d.) *The Living Seas* aquarium tank

Believe it or not, Bay Lake, the Seven Seas Lagoon, and even the World Showcase Lagoon are not nearly as deep as the 27-foot *Living Seas* tank. Bay Lake is just 12 feet deep, while the Seven Seas Lagoon and World Showcase Lagoon are 14 and 15 feet deep, respectively.

91. c.) 1994

The "Walk Around The World" promotion allowed Guests to purchase and personalize a hexagonal brick to be laid in a pathway leading almost all the way around the shores of the Seven Seas Lagoon, in front of the Magic Kingdom, the Transportation and Ticket Center, and Disney's Contemporary, Polynesian, and Grand Floridian Resort hotels. For approximately $100, a Guest could sponsor a brick, have it engraved with one of seven symbols (such as wedding bells, hearts or Mickey's head), and add up to three short lines of text. The bricks sold out in the year 2000, and there are no plans to add to the walkway. However, Guests can still become a permanent part of WDW by having their image engraved on one of Epcot's "Leave a Legacy" sculptures, located in front of *Spaceship Earth.*

92. c.) Main Street, U.S.A.
Located at the entrance to the Main Street Exposition Hall and Camera Center, the Goofy Pose-a-Matic was an odd-looking statue that was designed to look like an old camera that resembled Goofy. It made a fun prop for a picture.

93. d.) *Kali River Rapids*
Coronado Springs Resort's main pool has a five-story Mayan pyramid towering over it. Mexico's pavilion is shaped like a Mesoamerican-inspired pyramid, while the Imagination! Pavilion's structure contains two impressive glass pyramids.

94 a.) Blizzard Beach
Located in the Ski Patrol area of the Blizzard Beach Water Park, the Mount Gushmore Expedition Climbing Experience is an adventure you'll find nowhere else in WDW. Guests can literally scale the side of Mount Gushmore in this unique expedition, which includes some mountaineering training and climbing equipment. You have to be 9 or older and pay an additional fee to "Face the Slush and Climb Mount Gush!"

95. b.) $3.50 to $4.95
When WDW opened in 1971,

there were no such things as "Park Hoppers" or even annual passes. Instead of purchasing one ticket for admission to all of the rides in the park, you paid an admission price and then had to buy individual tickets, or books of tickets, to ride most attractions. For $3.50 you could enter the Magic Kingdom and experience the free attractions (yes, some were free, believe it or not). For a $4.95 admission, you also got an Adult 7-Ride Coupon Book that contained a mix of A, B, C, D, and E tickets. Additional tickets cost 25 to 50 cents each. The best attractions, such as *The Haunted Mansion,* required an E ticket.

96. b.) *Reflections of China*
China has changed tremendously since Epcot opened in 1982, so it was only fitting that Disney should update the long-running Circle-Vision 360 film in the China pavilion. Thus in 2003, the film that had been showing at Epcot since the park opened was completely redone. The new film showcases a more modern China, including views of Hong Kong, the Forbidden City, and Shanghai. Poet Li Bai, who narrated the original *Wonders of China* film, also narrates this one.

97. a.) The Bill Windsor family
Lakeland, Florida residents Marty and Bill Windsor, Jr., with their sons, Jay and Lee, were the first

family to walk through the gates on WDW's Opening Day in 1971.

98. c.) Disney-MGM Studios

Prior to the opening of *Fantasmic!*, the nighttime fireworks show presented at the Studios was known as *Sorcery in the Sky*. It featured a 55-foot inflatable Mickey Mouse rising above the Chinese Theater, with fireworks shooting out from his pointing finger. Accompanied by music from more than a dozen classic and modern movies, this spectacular live-action laser and fireworks show ran from 1990 to 1998.

99. b.) Reedy Creek Improvement District

The District is a private corporation that is located in both Orange and Osceola counties and contains two tiny towns, Lake Buena Vista and Bay Lake. Disney created Reedy Creek primarily to allow it to exercise governmental control over the land that constitutes WDW. This gives Disney the power, should it decide to exercise it, to levy taxes and even raise funds through the sale of tax-free municipal bonds. It also gives Disney the power to create and enforce its own building codes. (Could you see getting approval for building a Castle or "mountain"?)

100. d.) *Sounds Dangerous*

At the beginning of the show, the Director, Sharon Brooks, lets Guests know that they'll be following an undercover police officer who is equipped with a spy camera.

101. d.) *Walt Disney World Railroad*

Wondering how you can choose your own ending on the *WDWRR*? It's easy — you can get off at the station of your choice. *Horizons*, the now-defunct attraction that used to be located in Epcot, actually did allow Guests to select one of three different endings to their ride. By pushing a button in their ride car, they could choose to travel via hovercraft, a submarine, or a space shuttle to return to the present. OK . . . OK . . . I guess technically you "choose your own ending" when you decide to leave Tom Sawyer Island, but your visit always ends the same way — you have to take the raft to leave the island — so it doesn't count.

102. c.) *Pirates of the Caribbean*

This phrase can be seen on the brass placard on a pole outside the entrance to the attraction. The full sign reads "Pirates of the Caribbean – Sail with the Tide. A thrilling adventure through dark mysterious caverns where 'dead men tell no tales.' See fun-loving pirates sack and burn a Caribbean seaport. Caribbean Plaza. Walt Disney World."

103. b.) *DINOSAUR*

Located in Disney's Animal Kingdom, *DINOSAUR* takes you on a fast-paced journey back in time. It truly is fast, a blast, and in the past!

104. c.) Club Cool

Club Cool, located in Epcot's Future World near Innoventions West, is not an attraction per se, but it is a great place to beat the summer heat and sample free (that's right, FREE!) Coca-Cola brand soft drinks from eight nations around the world. Among the flavors on tap: "Beverly" (a bitter pre-dinner appetite stimulant from Italy), "Kinley Lemon" (an Israeli drink made from lemons, water, and honey that was popular as far back as the 12th century, when Genghis Khan's warriors quaffed it), "Krest Ginger Ale" (a popular drink in Mozambique bars, called shebeens, where it is used as a mixer), "Mezzo Mix" (a German drink that tastes a little like regular Coca-Cola and is often mixed with beer to weaken the alcohol content), "Smart Watermelon" (from China, which produces 40% of the world's watermelon crop), and "Vegitabeta" (a vitamin-rich drink that's popular in Japan, where it is dispensed from "Health" vending machines).

105. d.) Epcot

Combining Christmas lighting with the sounds of traditional carols and modern holiday classics, the "Lights of Winter" is on display from Thanksgiving through New Year's Day on archways lining the walkway between Future World and World Showcase. The archways are festooned with blinking lights and wired to broadcast the joyful music of the season.

106. a.) *The Enchanted Tiki Room – Under New Management*

Comedian Don Rickles (Mr. Potato Head from the *Toy Story* movies) is the voice of William in the pre-show of *The Enchanted Tiki Room*.

107. c.) Whispering Canyon Café

Guests can dine with Goofy, Minnie, and Chip and Dale at the Cape May Café in Disney's Beach Club resort. They can also dine daily with Christopher Robin's pals at a Winnie the Pooh Character Buffet at The Crystal Palace in the Magic Kingdom. Those who prefer to dine with a princess should head for Epcot's Norway pavilion. Restaurant Akershus was formally renamed Akershus Royal Banquet Hall in 2005, when it began hosting princess character meals at breakfast, lunch, and dinner.

108. b.) The WDW Dolphin

The WDW Dolphin, located close to Epcot and the Studios, offers 1,509 guest rooms. Its main building is 27 stories high.

109. c.) CommuniCore East

Located in the northeast quadrant of

Did You Know?

CAST MEMBERS PLAYING SNOW WHITE AND ARIEL
ARE NOT ALLOWED TO GET A TAN, EVEN WHEN THEY
ARE "OFF DUTY." SNOW WHITE CAN'T BECAUSE
SHE MUST HAVE FAIR SKIN, AND ARIEL CAN'T
BECAUSE MERMAIDS DON'T HAVE TAN LINES.

the former CommuniCore buildings were EPCOT Computer Central, Travelport, the Stargate Restaurant, and the Energy Exchange. The last was a hands-on exhibit sponsored by Exxon that looked at the future of fuel, alternative energy sources such as solar and wind power, and ways to conserve energy. Among the hands-on exhibits was a computer simulation that showed you how the choices you make when driving a car affect gas consumption. Energy Exchange closed on January 31, 1994, when the CommuniCore buildings closed for renovation.

110. b.) *Davy Crockett and the River Pirates*

The *Mike Fink Keelboats* once traveled the Rivers of America in the MK and were inspired by the 1955 Disneyland TV show and 1956 film, *Davy Crockett and the River Pirates*, in which Mike Fink, "King of the River," and Davy Crockett, "King of the Wild Frontier," had a keelboat race down the Mississippi river in two boats, the *Gullywhumper* and the *Bertha Mae*. In the B-ticket WDW attraction, boats of the same names docked at a small landing near *The Haunted Mansion*. From there, the boats took Guests on a leisurely cruise around Tom Sawyer Island, much like the *Liberty Belle* does today. The *Mike Fink Keelboats* attraction first opened in Disneyland, and the *Bertha Mae* and the *Gullywhumper* used there were the actual boats used in the film.

111. d.) *The Great Movie Ride*
Your Cast Member tour guide gives you this warning as you enter the *Alien* scene. He or she is right, too! Look out for the alien!

Did You Know?

THE TOTAL VOLUME OF WATER IN BAY LAKE AND ADJOINING SEVEN SEAS LAGOON IS, OH, JUST AROUND 2.385 BILLION (THAT'S 2,385,000,000) GALLONS.

112. a.) *Tower of Terror*
In the library pre-show, you can hear the Rod Serling impersonator say, "Amid the glitz and the glitter of a bustling, young movie town at the height of its golden age, The Hollywood Tower Hotel was a star in its own right; a beacon for the show business elite. Now, something is about to happen that will change all that."

113. b.) Buddy Ebsen
Walt wanted the Imagineers to duplicate human movements in a small figure using cams and wires. He hired Ebsen (best known as the star of the *Beverly Hillbillies* and *Barnaby Jones* TV shows) to dance for the Imagineers so that they could try to simulate his movements. The scale model of the stage and figure they built can be seen at the Studios' *Walt Disney: One Man's Dream* exhibit.

114. d.) A World Showcase pavilion
As part of Disney's 15-month Millennium Celebration at Epcot, Disney created a Millennium Village pavilion in World Showcase. The 65,000-square-foot building housed over 50 nations from around the world that were not previously represented in WS, featuring educational, cultural, and historical exhibits from such nations as Brazil, Chile, South Africa, Scotland, Sweden, Saudi Arabia, and Israel. In addition to enjoying hands-on exhibits and talking with international goodwill ambassadors, Guests could create their own keepsakes through pin trading and sample exotic cuisine in one of eight different kitchens. The building now houses special events and corporate functions.

115. a.) *The Great Movie Ride*
The initials "C.B." are a tribute to legendary director and producer Cecil B. DeMille and to the famous movie line: "I'm ready for my close-up, Mr. DeMille," spoken by Gloria Swanson in Billy Wilder's *Sunset Boulevard*.

116. c.) *Carousel of Progress*
In the first scene, circa 1900, Jimmy, the son, can be seen using a stereo-

scope next to an oil lamp. The father scolds him for not asking permission first, and Jimmy retorts, "Ooh la la! So that's the Norwegian doing the hoochie-coochie, eh Dad?"

117. b.) Construct a nuclear power plant

Disney's agreement with the city of Orlando and the state of Florida allows it to exercise quasi-governmental powers over the area in which WDW is located. This gives Disney the autonomy to implement its own schools, justice system, and even build its own nuclear power plant, should it ever choose to do so.

118. d.) PeopleMovers

Problems with transportation, including pollution and congestion, were just a few of the issues Walt wanted to eliminate in his city of tomorrow. To that end, he designed a "Transportation Lobby" that would be hidden underground, beneath his 30-story hotel. This terminal would serve both residents and visitors. Walt also wanted two separate but interconnected electrically powered transit systems, a high-speed monorail for rapid transit over longer distances, and a WEDway PeopleMover for shorter hauls. (Both systems are currently in place in WDW, although not as he originally imagined them.) Cars and trucks would have been allowed in Walt's EPCOT, but they would have

traveled on roadways sunk below the pedestrian level.

119. c.) Protecting the Magic

The motto of the Reedy Creek Fire Department, "Protecting the Magic," matches its job — protecting almost 40 square miles (25,000 acres) in the cities of Lake Buena Vista and Bay Lake that comprises all the WDW theme parks, resorts, roadways, and surrounding areas. The Department operates out of four fire stations with three engine companies, two tower trucks, and seven ALS (Advanced Life Support) ambulances among its fleet of support vehicles. In addition to handling fires, it provides a 911 communications center as well as emergency medical treatment and transport.

120. d.) Captain EO's crew

The crew in the 3-D musical sci-fi adventure known as *Captain EO* consisted of Hooter, Fuzzball, the Geex (Idy and Ody), Major Domo, and Minor Domo. Captain EO and his crew land on an oppressed planet to rescue the inhabitants from the Supreme Leader through music, dance, and light.

121. a.) Magic Kingdom

Thought it was *Tower of Terror*, *Rock 'n' Roller Coaster* or *Mission: SPACE* that has the tallest height requirement? Think again! The

Magic Kingdom's *Tomorrowland Indy Speedway* requires drivers to be at least 52 inches tall, although a passenger of any height is allowed to ride. Wondering about the other parks? The Studios' *Rock 'n' Roller Coaster* and DAK's *Primeval Whirl* require riders to be at least 48 inches, tall while Epcot's *Mission: SPACE* has a 44-inch height restriction.

122. c.) Rosie's All American Café
Located on Sunset Boulevard near Catalina Eddie's at the Studios, this counter-service restaurant serves burgers, sandwiches, salads, soup, and more.

123. a.) *Test Track*
Signs bearing this motto were found in the queue lines outside the *Test Track* building more than a year before it opened to the public in 1999. In fact, it opened almost a year and a half behind schedule.

124. b.) *The Wonderful World of Water Ski Show*
This show ran on the Seven Seas Lagoon five times daily during the summers of 1972 and 1973. Guests needed a D ticket to watch it from a special viewing area. Kite acts, water skiers, and even water-skiing characters such as Goofy and Donald were part of the short-lived production.

125. b.) *DINOSAUR*
Dr. Seeker says this during the pre-show, after he decides to go through with his secret plan of getting you to go back in time and bring him back a dinosaur.

126. d.) *Jungle Cruise*
Don't know what or who "Irrawaddy" or "Wamba" are? All of the boats in WDW's *Jungle Cruise* are named after rivers of the world. Although there are a total of 16 boats in the fleet, no more than 12 can be on the river at one time, including 3 at the loading dock. Here are all the boat names: *Amazon Annie, Bomokandi Bertha, Congo Connie, Ganges Gertie, Irrawaddy Irma, Kwango Kate, Mongala Millie, Nile Nellie, Orinoco Ida, Rutshuru Ruby, Sankuru Sadie, Senegal Sal, Ucayali Lolly, Volta Val, Wamba Wanda,* and *Zambezi Zelda.*

Did You Know?

WDW PURCHASES MORE THAN 3.8 MILLION PENS EVERY YEAR.

127. a.) America Gardens Theater in Epcot

In 1993, *The Magical World of Barbie* stage show premiered at the America Gardens Theater in front of the U.S.A. pavilion. The 20-minute production was presented by Mattel and featured Barbie and her friends taking a musical trip around the world, with a final stop in Paris for a fashion show. Barbie, dubbed the "Ambassador of Friendship," arrived at the show in a long pink stretch limo, which was originally created for Mickey's 60th birthday party. Guests could meet and greet her and her friend Ken by the limo and pose for pictures with them. The show ended with a fireworks display and the release of white doves. (Not at the same time, of course.)

128. c.) Rivers of America

Located in the middle of the Rivers of America in Frontierland, the former South Island is now nameless and there are no references to it on current guide maps. However, you may very well visit it when you're at the Magic Kingdom. You see, Tom Sawyer "Island" is actually a misnomer — the attraction now comprises two islands (connected by a long suspension bridge), one of them the former South Island. That wasn't always the case: When Tom Sawyer Island opened in 1973, the islands were unconnected and South Island wasn't part of the attraction.

129. b.) *Journey Into Imagination*

General Electric has sponsored a number of Disney attractions and projects, among them: *Horizons, Carousel of Progress,* the original *IllumiNations,* and the addition of lighting to most of the pavilions in Epcot's World Showcase. GE, along with other companies, also showcases products that you may find in the home of the future in Innoventions East Side.

130. c.) *Back to Neverland*

This 9-minute film could once be seen in the "The Magic of Disney Animation" tour in Disney-MGM Studios. *Back to Neverland* (where Robin Williams coincidentally went in the 1991 film *Hook*) played at the Studios from its opening in 1989 until 2004, when it was shelved for good because the characters (and Walter Cronkite) were unfamiliar to younger Guests and had become somewhat dated.

131. a.) Delta Airlines

Eastern Airlines was the first "official" airline of WDW and sponsored one of the MK's early attractions, *If You Had Wings.* Its sponsorship ended in 1987, and the attraction was closed temporarily to remove all references to Eastern and change the attraction's name to *If You Could Fly.* When Delta became the sponsor in 1989, a new attraction opened under the name of Delta's *Dreamflight.*

creation of a 1930s British Explorers Club, where you journey from room to room to experience outrageous songs, jokes, and tales told by zany explorers.

133. a.) *The Glory and Pageantry of Christmas*
Beginning in 1978, Disney presented a live nativity display called *The Glory and Pageantry of Christmas*. The show ran for 17 years at the Disney Village Marketplace (now known as Downtown Disney). It was replaced in 1995 with *Tropical Santa*, which included a tree lighting ceremony, carolers, a musical stage show, Caribbean renditions of classic Christmas carols, a lighted boat parade, a sing-along, and fireworks.

134. a.) A permanent residential community
In June 1973, Disney announced plans for a residential community that was to be built on WDW property and known as "Lake Buena Vista." The community would contain townhouses in four themed areas: Golf, Tennis, Boating, and Western. By May 1974, 133 townhouses had been built and the nearby Lake Buena Vista Village shopping and dining complex was under construction. Plans were also underway to build single-family houses, apartments, and condominiums. When the shopping village opened in March 1975, however, not a single

Delta was named the second official airline of WDW in 1995, but Delta and Disney severed their relationship a few years later, and *Dreamflight* became *Take Flight*. Disney has no official airline as we go to press.

132. b.) Adventurers Club
You'll find the "Come in a Stranger, Leave a Little Stranger" sign at the entrance to the Adventurers Club in Pleasure Island. An "Open House," dated 1937, invites you into this re-

villa was on the market and no houses or apartments were under construction. What happened to the plans for a permanent community? Disney had overlooked a major issue: permanent residents would have had to be granted voting rights on such issues as taxation, construction, budgets, and more, and Disney decided it didn't want that many fingers in its pie. (This was also one of the reasons the EPCOT residential community Walt had envisioned failed to materialize and why, after Disney finally built the permanent residential community of Celebration in 1994, it later spun some of it off.)

135. b.) *The Timekeeper*
At the very end of the attraction, Timekeeper told you that the show was over and that he had to go do a few things, like give Sigmund Freud a piece of his mind ("Oedipus Schmedipus!").

136. c.) *Frontierland Shootin' Arcade*
You can find "Ruthless Billy Jack" (sort of) on Boot Hill at the *Frontierland Shootin' Arcade*. According to his tombstone, he "bit the bullet" on February 13. You can see the date if you hit his tombstone.

137. a.) *America the Beautiful*
This first Circle-Vision film to be shown in WDW opened November 25, 1971. The first new attraction to open in Tomorrowland, it joined the *Grand Prix Raceway* and the *Skyway to Fantasyland*. The film was replaced by *Magic Carpet 'Round the World* from 1974 to 1975 while *America the Beautiful* was being updated to include footage for the nation's upcoming Bicentennial. It reopened in 1975 and played through 1979. *Magic Carpet 'Round the World* returned in 1979 and ran for 5 more years. On September 15, 1984, it was replaced by *American Journeys*, which was itself replaced by *The Timekeeper* on January 9, 1994.

138. c.) *Swiss Family Treehouse*
On the sign for the Library, you will find, "These good books – the recordings of man's ideas and achievements were salvaged from our ship. We shall never hunger of food for the mind nor the soul."

Signed, Franz R.

Did You Know?

CINDERELLA CASTLE WAS INSPIRED BY A NUMBER OF
EUROPEAN CASTLES, INCLUDING CHENONCEAU IN
FRANCE. BUT UNLIKE THAT SIXTEENTH-CENTURY
CHATEAU, CINDERELLA CASTLE WAS BUILT WITH
600 TONS OF STEEL AND NOT A SINGLE STONE.

CHAPTER TWO

MAGIC KINGDOM

1. The Magic Kingdom was dedicated on ___?
- a.) October 1, 1971
- b.) October 25, 1971
- c.) October 1, 1972
- d.) When groundbreaking began in 1967

2. What attraction is based on Walt Disney's very first full-length animated classic?
- a.) *Snow White's Scary Adventures*
- b.) *Peter Pan's Flight*
- c.) *Cinderella's Golden Carrousel*
- d.) *Dumbo the Flying Elephant*

3. In which of these attractions could you NOT hear Thurl Ravenscroft, the man who sang "You're a Mean One, Mr. Grinch"?
- a.) *Country Bear Jamboree*
- b.) *If You Had Wings*
- c.) *The Haunted Mansion*
- d.) *Tropical Serenade*

Did You Know?

NO GASOLINE-POWERED VEHICLES ARE ALLOWED IN THE TUNNELS BELOW THE MAGIC KINGDOM — EXCEPT ONE: AN ARMORED CAR THAT PICKS UP THE CASH COLLECTED EACH DAY. BUT IT'S A TIGHT FIT: THE DRIVER HAS ONLY FOUR INCHES ON EITHER SIDE IN WHICH TO MANEUVER THE VEHICLE.

0	1	2	3	4

4. How far does Tinker Bell "fly" during her flight from Cinderella Castle?
a.) 155 feet
b.) 375 feet
c.) 500 feet
d.) 750 feet

5. What was the first new attraction to open after the MK's Opening Day?
a.) *Peter Pan's Flight*
b.) *The Haunted Mansion*
c.) *Liberty Square Riverboat*
d.) *"it's a small world"*

6. Where could you find the Lancer's Inn?
a.) Fantasyland
b.) Frontierland
c.) Liberty Square
d.) Adventureland

7. An engine named after which of these people was introduced to the *WDW Railroad* in the 1990s?
a.) Lillian Disney
b.) Ward Kimball
c.) Samuel Clemens
d.) Roger E. Broggie

8. What replaced the *Main Street Electrical Parade*?
a.) *Fantasmic!*
b.) *Share a Dream Come True Parade*
c.) *The Magic Kingdom Parade*
d.) *SpectroMagic*

9. What Audio-Animatronics show was led by "Maestro Mickey"?
a.) *Mickey Mouse Revue*
b.) *Mickey's Toontown Cabaret*
c.) *The Diamond Horseshoe Revue*
d.) *Mickey's PhilharMagic*

10. The *Plaza Swan Boats* were a ___ ticket attraction?
a.) B
b.) C
c.) D
d.) E

11. Which of these lands cannot be reached directly from the central hub in front of Cinderella Castle?
a.) Tomorrowland
b.) Frontierland
c.) Adventureland
d.) Liberty Square

12. What Magic Kingdom attraction was discovered in Mexico?
a.) *Tom Sawyer Island*
b.) *Mike Fink Keelboats*
c.) *Cinderella's Golden Carrousel*
d.) *WDW Railroad*

13. On the statue of Walt and Mickey in front of Cinderella Castle, Walt is wearing a tie clip with the initials "STR" on it. What does STR stand for?
a.) Save The Rainforests
b.) Smoke Tree Ranch
c.) See The Rainbow
d.) A Chinese phrase that means "Peace, love and family"

14. Where can you find a Chinese restaurant in the Magic Kingdom?
a.) Liberty Square
b.) Adventureland
c.) Frontierland
d.) Main Street, U.S.A.

15. Who cut the ribbon for the Grand Opening of Mickey's Birthdayland?
a.) Cindy Williams
b.) Penny Marshall
c.) Robin Williams
d.) Chevy Chase

16. The first riverboat to ply the Rivers of America was ___?

a.) *Richard F. Irvine*
b.) *Liberty Belle*
c.) *Admiral Joe Fowler*
d.) *Lillian Belle*

17. How many passenger cars are there on each *WDW Railroad* train?
a.) 5
b.) 4
c.) 3
d.) 2

18. Who is the "narrator" of the *Wishes* fireworks show?
a.) Tinker Bell
b.) Jiminy Cricket
c.) Mickey Mouse
d.) The Genie from *Aladdin*

19. Which of these attractions had its track shortened in 1988?
a.) *Space Mountain*
b.) *WDW Railroad*
c.) *Grand Prix Raceway*
d.) *Pirates of the Caribbean*

20. What is the oldest ride in the Magic Kingdom?
a.) *WDW Railroad*
b.) *The Haunted Mansion*
c.) *Liberty Square Riverboat*
d.) *Cinderella's Golden Carrousel*

21. How many people can the Magic Kingdom park hold?
a.) 15,000
b.) 50,000
c.) 75,000
d.) 100,000

Did You Know?

DON'T ASK ME HOW I KNOW THIS, OR HOW THEY FIGURED THIS OUT, BUT … IF YOU STACKED ALL OF THE BUTTONS USED BY THE COSTUMING PLANT SEAM TEAM IN ONE YEAR, THE STACK WOULD BE MORE THAN 96 TIMES AS TALL AS CINDERELLA CASTLE.

22. One of the *WDW Railroad*'s steam engines has a whistle sound that is unlike the others. Which one is it?

a.) *Lilly Belle*
b.) *Walter E. Disney*
c.) *Roy O. Disney*
d.) *Roger E. Broggie*

23. What is the promenade between Tomorrowland and the MK's central hub called?

a.) Avenue of Tomorrow
b.) WED Way
c.) Tomorrowland Turnpike
d.) Avenue of the Planets

24. When WDW was being designed and developed, there were plans for rides based on all of these characters EXCEPT ___?

a.) Sleeping Beauty
b.) Mary Poppins
c.) Mr. Toad
d.) Ichabod Crane

25. What celebrity's voice could be heard in the now-defunct *If You Had Wings* attraction?

a.) John Wayne
b.) Orson Welles
c.) John Forsythe
d.) Lorne Greene

26. Which of these attractions was operational on the MK's Opening Day?

a.) *If You Had Wings*
b.) *20,000 Leagues Under the Sea*
c.) *Carousel of Progress*
d.) *Skyway*

27. Casey's Corner was originally named:
a.) Refreshment Corner
b.) Pluto's Hot Dogs
c.) Plaza Pavilion
d.) Mickey's Mart

28. What is the elevation of the Magic Kingdom?
a.) 18 feet
b.) 108 feet
c.) 1971 feet
d.) "Endless"

29. Who presents the MK's *Share a Dream Come True* parade?
a.) Mattel
b.) Nestlé
c.) Kodak
d.) McDonald's

30. Which of these attractions originally required reservations?
a.) *The Diamond Horseshoe Revue*
b.) *The Enchanted Tiki Room*
c.) *Country Bear Jamboree*
d.) *Hall of Presidents*

31. On what body of water could you have found the *Richard F. Irvine*, the *Gullywhumper*, and the *Bertha Mae*?
a.) Bay Lake
b.) Seven Seas Lagoon

c.) Rivers of America
d.) Lake Buena Vista

32. About how fast does the *WDW Railroad* travel?
a.) 10 mph
b.) 20 mph
c.) 30 mph
d.) 40 mph

33. Which of these attractions was NOT an E-ticket ride?
a.) *Jungle Cruise*
b.) *Hall of Presidents*
c.) *20,000 Leagues Under the Sea*
d.) *Peter Pan's Flight*

34. What year did the *Skyway* close?
a.) 1979
b.) 1987
c.) 1989
d.) 1999

35. In 2005, a new door with a windowpane was installed on a building on Main Street, U.S.A. Who is honored in that window?
a.) Cast Members
b.) Joe Rohde
c.) All WDW's returning Guests
d.) Michael Eisner

36. Can you name the MK's most technologically advanced parade to date?
a.) *Main Street Electrical Parade*
b.) *SpectroMagic*
c.) *Share a Dream Come True*
d.) *Tapestry of Dreams*

Did You Know?

ON A WALL INSIDE CINDERELLA CASTLE YOU'LL FIND A MOSAIC SHOWING CINDERELLA'S STEPSISTERS. ONE'S FACE IS RED WITH ANGER, WHILE THE OTHER'S IS GREEN WITH ENVY.

37. About how many passengers per year ride the *WDW Railroad*?
  a.) 500,000
  b.) 1,000,000
  c.) 2,000,000
  d.) 3,000,000

Main Street, U.S.A.

38. What town inspired the design of Main Street, U.S.A.?
  a.) Marceline, Missouri
  b.) Chicago, Illinois
  c.) Kansas City, Missouri
  d.) Point Pleasant, New Jersey

39. Main Street, U.S.A. is how many blocks long?
  a.) 1
  b.) 2
  c.) 3
  d.) 4

40. The double-decker bus that used to transport Guests down Main Street, U.S.A. was the ___?
  a.) Dapper Dan's Town Tour
  b.) Magic Tours
  c.) Main Street Trolley
  d.) Omnibus

41. What was the name of the now-defunct magic shop on Main Street, U.S.A.?
  a.) Houdini's
  b.) Mickey's Magic Shop
  c.) House of Magic
  d.) Tricks and Treats

42. Who is the Mayor of Main Street, U.S.A.?
  a.) Mickey Mouse
  b.) George Weaver
  c.) Walt Disney
  d.) I. M. Running

43. Which of these companies once sponsored an attraction on Main Street, U.S.A.?
  a.) Gulf Oil
  b.) Enron
  c.) AT&T
  d.) Microsoft

44. What is the name of the statue

located in the center of Town Square on Main Street, U.S.A.?
- a.) *Partners*
- b.) *Dreams Come True*
- c.) *Remember the Magic*
- d.) *Sharing the Magic*

45. The area located under the Main Street Railroad Station (where the lockers used to be) is called ___?
- a.) Main Street Station House
- b.) Harmony House
- c.) Station Break
- d.) Whistle Stop

46. You can enjoy what barber-shop quartet on Main Street, U.S.A.?
- a.) The Mello Men
- b.) The Dapper Dans
- c.) The Step Tones
- d.) ChordiNation Quartet

47. You'll find how many places to eat on Main Street, U.S.A.?
- a.) 16
- b.) 13
- c.) 8
- d.) 2

48. Which of these shops was NOT found on Main Street, U.S.A.?
- a.) Tobacconist
- b.) Holiday Corner
- c.) Main Street Book Store
- d.) Main Street Candy Station

49. Above what building on Main Street, U.S.A. does Walt Disney's name appear?
- a.) Exhibition Hall
- b.) Tony's Town Square
- c.) Plaza Ice Cream Parlor
- d.) The Crystal Palace

Adventureland

50. According to the sign out front, in what year was the *Swiss Family Treehouse* built?

Did You Know?

THE IMAGINEERS ORIGINALLY WANTED TO PAVE MAIN STREET, U.S.A. ENTIRELY WITH BRICKS. BUT THE PRICE FOR THE BRICKS THEY FOUND WAS TOO HIGH, SO THEY ONLY USED BRICKS ON THE SIDE STREETS AND PAVED MAIN STREET WITH RED CEMENT.

Did You Know?

THE HORSE-SHAPED HITCHING POSTS ON MAIN STREET, U.S.A. ARE SCRAPED AND REPAINTED TWICE A MONTH!

a.) 1779
b.) 1805
c.) 1929
d.) 1971

51. How many attractions did Adventureland offer on Opening Day in 1971?
a.) 1
b.) 2
c.) 3
d.) 4

52. What did Walt Disney originally want the *Jungle Cruise* to contain?
a.) A flume
b.) Boats that the guests could control on their own
c.) Live animals
d.) Characters from some Disney animated features

53. Which of the following animals adorns the Swiss Family Robinson's family crest?
a.) Eagle
b.) Bear

c.) Elephant
d.) Cat

54. Who is the Tiki god that Iago upsets in *The Enchanted Tiki Room – Under New Management*?
a.) Zazu
b.) Uhoa
c.) Vulcania
d.) Catalina

55. What Adventureland attraction was originally conceived as a dinner-theater show?
a.) *The Enchanted Tiki Room*
b.) *Pirates of the Caribbean*
c.) *Swiss Family Treehouse*
d.) *Jungle Cruise*

56. It may be a pirate's life for me, but about how long is the actual boat ride in *Pirates of the Caribbean*?
a.) 4 minutes
b.) 10 minutes
c.) 16 minutes
d.) 21 minutes

57. How are the boats powered in the *Jungle Cruise*?
- a.) Propane
- b.) Gasoline engines
- c.) Steam engines
- d.) Natural gas

58. Which current WDW attraction premiered in Disneyland in 1963 and was the first to use Audio-Animatronics figures?
- a.) *The Enchanted Tiki Room*
- b.) *Pirates of the Caribbean*
- c.) *The Haunted Mansion*
- d.) *Country Bear Jamboree*

59. Who is the second "barker bird" who stood outside *The Enchanted Tiki Room*, singing and directing guests into the attraction?
- a.) Orange Julius
- b.) The Orange Bird
- c.) Artemus
- d.) Cornelius

60. What type of "tree" houses the Swiss Family Robinson?
- a.) Banyan
- b.) Disneyodendron
- c.) Swiss oak
- d.) Floridian spruce

61. Which of these rivers do you travel along LAST during your voyage on the *Jungle Cruise*?
- a.) Mekong
- b.) Amazon
- c.) Congo
- d.) Nile

62. What is one way the signs for the *Swiss Family Treehouse* differed in WDW and Disneyland?
- a.) The shipwreck dates differed.
- b.) The wife was named in one but not the other.
- c.) The word "uncharted" did not appear on Disneyland's sign.
- d.) The ships' names differed.

Frontierland

63. Who is the Marshall of Frontierland?

Did You Know?

THE NAMES OF THE TWO CROCODILES YOU MEET ON THE *JUNGLE CRUISE* ARE OL' SMILEY AND GINGER. DON'T FORGET THAT "GINGER SNAPS."

Did You Know?

a.) Jack Dalton
b.) Gus Johnson
c.) Slingin' Sam Jones
d.) Wild Willie Washington

64. In the *Country Bear Jamboree*, which bear plays the mouth harp?
a.) Teddi Barra
b.) Liver Lips
c.) Big Al
d.) Fred

65. How high is the drop on *Splash Mountain*?
a.) 1 story
b.) 3 stories
c.) 5 stories
d.) 7 stories

66. According to the sign, what's the population of the fictitious town through which the *Big Thunder Mountain Railroad* runs?
a.) 1
b.) 1,971
c.) "A whole bunch of critters, and little else"
d.) "Dried out"

67. Which restaurant is located on Tom Sawyer Island?

a.) Aunt Polly's Dockside Inn
b.) Huck's Homestyle Cookin'
c.) Columbia Harbour House
d.) There is no restaurant on the island.

68. Who is the host of the *Country Bear Jamboree*?
a.) Big Al
b.) Henry
c.) Max
d.) Buff

69. On Big Thunder Mountain, what is the name of the town your train passes through?
a.) Death Valley
b.) Tumbleweed
c.) Boom Town
d.) Sam's Town

70. What year did Tom Sawyer Island open?
a.) 1971
b.) 1972
c.) 1973
d.) 1981

71. Which of these states is also the name of a bear in the WDW *Country Bear Jamboree*?

a.) Alabama

b.) Tennessee

c.) Georgia

d.) Texas

72. What event destroyed the mining town on Big Thunder Mountain?

a.) Flash flood

b.) Earthquake

c.) Train crash

d.) The mines ran dry

73. Can you name the song performed by Big Al in the *Country Bear Jamboree*?

a.) "My Woman Ain't Pretty, But She Don't Swear None"

b.) "Blood on the Saddle"

c.) "The Ballad of Davy Crockett"

d.) "He's Big Around the Middle and He's Broad Across the Rump"

74. *Splash Mountain* is based on what Disney film?

a.) *Brother Bear*

b.) *Song of the South*

c.) *Davy Crockett and the River Pirates*

d.) *Johnny Tremain*

75. Which of the following is NOT one of the names of the rafts that transport you to Tom Sawyer Island?

a.) Tom Sawyer

b.) Injun Joe

c.) Becky Thatcher

d.) Sam Clemens

76. How many people per train can ride *Big Thunder Mountain Railroad*?

a.) 10

b.) 20

c.) 30

d.) 40

77. Which of these was a proposed name for *Splash Mountain*?

a.) Splash Down

b.) The Zip-A-Dee-Doo-Dah River Run

c.) Brer Mountain

d.) Song of the South River Adventure

78. Do you know the original name of Fort Langhorn on Tom Sawyer Island?

a.) Fort Huckleberry

b.) Fort Freedom

c.) Fort Sam Clemens

d.) Fort Wilderness

79. What was the name of the proposed Frontierland attraction that prompted the eventual building of the *Big Thunder Mountain Railroad*?

a.) *Western River Expedition*

b.) *Legend of the Runaway Train*

c.) *American Frontiers*

d.) *Pioneer Gold Rush Adventure*

Liberty Square

80. According to the crypt outside the exit to *The Haunted Mansion*, which of Bluebeard's wives "did him in"?
- a.) Penelope
- b.) Lucretia
- c.) Eugenia
- d.) Abigail

81. What was the name of the patriotic ceremony held daily in Liberty Square?
- a.) Voices of Liberty
- b.) The Sons and Daughters of Liberty
- c.) American Dreams
- d.) A Tribute to Freedom

82. Who had a great big rock fall on his head according to the gravestones at *The Haunted Mansion*?
- a.) Master Gracey
- b.) Martin

- c.) Dave
- d.) Fred

83. WDW's *Hall of Presidents* was originally planned as a Disneyland attraction. What was the attraction's original proposed name?
- a.) *One Nation Under God*
- b.) *Sweet Land of Liberty*
- c.) *The Hall of Presidents*
- d.) *The American Adventure*

84. What are the names of the three hitchhiking ghosts in *The Haunted Mansion*?
- a.) Huey, Duey and Louie
- b.) Gus, Ezra and Phineas
- c.) Master Gracey, Tommy Tombs and Danny Dirtnap
- d.) Marco, Smokey and Cecil

85. The *Liberty Square Riverboat* is narrated by whom?
- a.) Tom Sawyer
- b.) Thomas Jefferson
- c.) Mark Twain
- d.) Paul Frees

Did You Know?

THE *COUNTRY BEAR JAMBOREE* IS AFFECTIONATELY KNOWN AS "WALT'S LAST LAUGH" AMONG IMAGINEERS, BECAUSE HE REVIEWED SKETCHES FOR THIS ATTRACTION AT THE IMAGINEERING OFFICES PRIOR TO HIS ADMISSION INTO THE HOSPITAL PRECEDING HIS DEATH.

Did You Know?

IF YOU LOOK UP TO THE TOP FLOOR OF
THE HAUNTED MANSION (ABOVE THE DOOR) WHEN
YOU'RE PASSING IT AT NIGHT, YOU JUST MIGHT SEE
TWO SHADOWS WALKING BY HOLDING A LANTERN.

86. What is the name of the ghost you encounter at the end of the attraction who encourages you to "make final arrangements" to remain in *The Haunted Mansion*?
- a.) Madame Leota
- b.) The Ghost Host
- c.) The Hitchhiking Ghosts
- d.) Little Leota

87. In what year was the Liberty Bell cast for placement in WDW?
- a.) 1971
- b.) 1983
- c.) 1989
- d.) 1999

88. Can you name the "owner" of *The Haunted Mansion*?
- a.) He is only known as "the groom."
- b.) Master Gracey
- c.) Master Hudson
- d.) Mister Walters

89. Other than in the White House in Washington, D.C., what object can be found only in WDW's *Hall of Presidents*?
- a.) A carpet containing the Presidential Seal
- b.) A signed copy of the Declaration of Independence
- c.) An original painting of George Washington
- d.) A pocket watch worn by Abraham Lincoln

90. Who is the voice of the Ghost Host in *The Haunted Mansion*?
- a.) Thurl Ravenscroft
- b.) Vincent Price
- c.) Paul Frees
- d.) Boris Karloff

91. What powers the *Liberty Square Riverboat*?
- a.) Pixie dust
- b.) Natural gas
- c.) Electricity
- d.) Steam

92. Who sings *The Haunted Mansion* theme song?
- a.) The Mello Men
- b.) The Haunted Mansion Players
- c.) Xavier Atencio
- d.) The Sherman Brothers

Did You Know?

THE *COUNTRY BEAR JAMBOREE*'S "BIG AL" WAS
MODELED AFTER IMAGINEER AL BERTINO,
WHO HELPED DESIGN AND WRITE THE SCRIPT
FOR THIS ATTRACTION AND NUMEROUS OTHERS.

Fantasyland

93. How many different songs play in the background of *Cinderella's Golden Carrousel?*
   a.) 6
   b.) 16
   c.) 26
   d.) 36

94. What pops out of the center teapot in the *Mad Tea Party?*
   a.) The Mad Hatter
   b.) A very dizzy Alice
   c.) Tweedle Dee and Tweedle Dum
   d.) A mouse

95. Where were you headed on *Mr. Toad's Wild Ride?*
   a.) Nowhere in Particular
   b.) London
   c.) Sleepy Hollow
   d.) Paris

96. In *"it's a small world,"* there are only two Audio-Animatronics figures that represent the United States. What are they?

   a.) A policeman and a fireman
   b.) A cowboy and an Indian
   c.) A football player and a baseball player
   d.) Frank Sinatra and Dean Martin

97. How many *Dumbo* ride cars were there before the attraction was renovated in 1993?
   a.) 8
   b.) 10
   c.) 14
   d.) 16

98. What is Cinderella's fountain in Fantasyland called?
   a.) "Magical Wishes"
   b.) "When You Wish Upon a Star"
   c.) "Glass Slipper"
   d.) "Rags to Riches"

99. In *Mickey's PhilharMagic*, what song does the orchestra continue playing, despite Donald's efforts to change its tune?
   a.) "The Mickey Mouse Club March"
   b.) "It's a Small World"

c.) "Minnie's Yoo Hoo"
d.) "Heigh Ho"

100. How many rows of horses are there on *Cinderella's Golden Carrousel*?
    a.) 3
    b.) 4
    c.) 5
    d.) 6

101. You'll find what on top of the hot air balloon at the center of *Dumbo the Flying Elephant*?
    a.) A pink ball
    b.) A baby elephant

c.) Clouds
d.) A mouse

102. *"it's a small world"* was originally the centerpiece of what pavilion in the 1964 World's Fair?
    a.) General Electric
    b.) UNICEF
    c.) Ford
    d.) The Disney Showcase

103. The *Mad Tea Party* ride has how many spinning teacups?
    a.) 12
    b.) 18
    c.) 20
    d.) 22

104. Only one nation's name is actually spelled out on the *"it's a small world"* attraction. What country is it?
    a.) Mexico
    b.) U.S.A.
    c.) China
    d.) Switzerland

105. What type of ticket did you need for *Mr. Toad's Wild Ride*?

Did You Know?

THE LIBERTY TREE IN LIBERTY SQUARE WAS INSPIRED BY A TREE IN THE 1957 DISNEY FILM *JOHNNY TREMAIN*. IN FACT, JOHNNY TREMAIN'S SILVER SHOPPE WAS ONCE LOCATED IN LIBERTY SQUARE, NEXT TO THE PERFUMERY.

a.) B
b.) C
c.) D
d.) E

106. How was *Snow White's Scary Adventures* changed in 1994?
a.) The wicked witch was removed from the ride.
b.) The ride carts were completely replaced.
c.) Many of the Audio-Animatronics figures were removed or replaced.
d.) Snow White was added to the attraction.

Mickey's Toontown Fair

107. What was Mickey's Toontown Fair originally called?
a.) It's always been Mickey's Toontown Fair.
b.) Mickey's Birthdayland
c.) Toon Town
d.) Mickey's Starland

108. *Mickey's Country House* has how many rooms?
a.) 3
b.) 4
c.) 5
d.) 6

109. What's the name of the farm on which *The Barnstormer*

attraction takes place?
a.) Mickey's Circle K Ranch
b.) Goofy's Wiseacre Farm
c.) Donald's Dairy Farm
d.) Minnie's Country Farmhouse

110. Who acts as Judge in Toontown?
a.) Mickey
b.) Minnie
c.) Cornelius Coot
d.) Goofy

111. What did *Minnie's Country House* replace?
a.) The Duckburg News store
b.) Mickey's Hollywood Theatre
c.) The Birthdayland Railroad Station
d.) Mouse-Ka-Maze

112. Which of these famous characters is NOT one of Mickey's pen pals?
a.) Peter Pan
b.) Buzz Lightyear
c.) Wendy
d.) Aladdin

113. Goofy's mailbox is located in front of *The Barnstormer*. What props the mailbox up?
a.) Stalks of corn
b.) A propeller
c.) A stack of tires
d.) His cousin

114. *Donald's Boat* is named ___?
a.) S.S. Donald

Did You Know?

A SPECIAL CREW POLISHES EVERY ONE OF THE
BRASS POLES ON *CINDERELLA'S GOLDEN CARROUSEL*
EVERY SINGLE NIGHT.

b.) Miss Fortune
c.) Miss Daisy
d.) Splash

115. What is the slogan on the front of Pete's Garage in Toontown?
  a.) "Trust Me With Your Car"
  b.) "If It Ain't Broke, I Can't Fix It"
  c.) "I Know What I'm Doing"
  d.) "If Your Car Is Really Broken, How Did You Drive It Here?"

116. Mickey's favorite football team plays for what school?

a.) Disney University
b.) Duckburg University
c.) Goofy University
d.) Toontown College

117. Which of these was the name of the little petting zoo that used to be found in Mickey's Toontown Fair?
  a.) *Petey's Petting Zoo*
  b.) *Grandma Duck's Farm*
  c.) *Goofy's Wiseacre Farm*
  d.) *Toontown Zoo*

118. Who drew the map inside the cabin of *Donald's Boat*?

a.) Ludwig von Drake
b.) Donald Duck
c.) Huey, Dewey and Louie
d.) Miss Daisy

119. What kind of table can you find in *Mickey's Country House*?
a.) Pool table
b.) Ping Pong table
c.) Foosball table
d.) Air hockey table

120. Which model plane do you travel in on Goofy's *Barnstormer*?
a.) Fearless Fido
b.) The Rubber Band Express
c.) El Cheapo
d.) Multiflex Octoplane

121. The statue in front of the *Toontown Hall of Fame* is perched upon ___?
a.) A soap box
b.) Ears of corn
c.) Pluto's doghouse
d.) A circus tent

122. Who moved next door to Mickey when Mickey's Toontown Fair opened?
a.) Goofy
b.) Minnie
c.) Donald
d.) His mother-in-law

123. What type of gas can you buy at Pete's Garage?
a.) Gulp Gas
b.) Pete's Petroleum

c.) Gotta Go Gas
d.) Exxon

124. What measurement scale is used for the plans for Mickey's automatic dishwasher?
a.) 1 pinch = 2 ouches
b.) 1 smidgen = 4 oodges
c.) 1 broken dish = 2 pieces of tape
d.) 1 foot = 5 toes

125. Prior to Mickey's Toontown Fair getting its current name, what was the name of the town where you could find Mickey's house?
a.) Mouseville
b.) Fantasia Gardens
c.) Duckburg
d.) Birthdayland

126. Water shoots out the top of *Donald's Boat* if you ___?
a.) Spin the wheel
b.) Ring the bell
c.) Open the door
d.) Pull a rope

127. Who is remodeling a room in *Mickey's Country House*?
a.) Mickey and Minnie
b.) Donald and Goofy
c.) Goofy and Minnie
d.) Donald's nephews

128. Goofy's *Barnstormer* is also the home of ___?
a.) Pete's Garage

Did You Know?

YOU CAN FIND CINDERELLA'S HORSE ON HER GOLDEN CARROUSEL IN FANTASYLAND! LOOK FOR THE STEED IN THE SECOND ROW FROM THE OUTSIDE WITH THE GOLDEN RIBBON ON ITS TAIL. THAT'S HERS!

b.) An airplane factory
c.) A flight school for pets
d.) A candy store

Tomorrowland

129. The renovated Tomorrowland opened in what year?
a.) 1995
b.) 1999
c.) 2000
d.) It has not been renovated since the park opened.

130. What is the dog's name in *Carousel of Progress?*
a.) Lucky
b.) Walt
c.) Rover
d.) Spot

131. Which of the following has never been shown in the Tomorrowland Circle-Vision Theatre?
a.) *The Timekeeper*
b.) *America the Beautiful*
c.) *Magic Carpet 'Round the World*
d.) *Magic Journeys*

132. The original sponsor of *Space Mountain* was ___?
a.) It had no sponsor.
b.) FedEx
c.) NASA
d.) RCA

133. What is the highest rank you can attain on *Buzz Lightyear's Space Ranger Spin?*
a.) Lieutenant Lightyear
b.) Galactic Hero
c.) Space Ace
d.) Captain Chaos

134. What type of ticket did you need in 1972 to ride *If You Had Wings?*
a.) A
b.) B
c.) C
d.) None

135. WDW's *Carousel of Progress* has how many theaters?
a.) 3
b.) 4
c.) 5
d.) 6

136. What attraction did *The ExtraTERRORestrial Alien Encounter* replace?
a.) *If You Had Wings*
b.) *Mission to Mars*
c.) *Flight to the Moon*
d.) *Dreamflight*

137. *Space Mountain* was originally going to be called ___?
a.) Star Gate
b.) Space Port
c.) Space Race
d.) Journey Into Tomorrow

138. According to a sign outside Metropolis Science Center, who conducts the Martian Pops Orchestra?

a.) Leonard Burnedstar
b.) Sonny Eclipse
c.) Martian Hamoonstein
d.) Tom Morrow

139. About how long is the actual ride in *Space Mountain*?
a.) 2 minutes, 30 seconds
b.) 4 minutes
c.) 6 minutes
d.) 7 minutes, 30 seconds

140. What was the name of the director of operations for *Flight to the Moon*?
a.) Mr. Johnson
b.) Sonny Eclipse
c.) Tom Morrow
d.) Captain EO

141. Sonny Eclipse is from ___?
a.) Yensid City
b.) Marceline, Missouri
c.) Endor
d.) Yew Nork City

142. What attraction did *American Journeys* replace?
a.) *If You Had Wings*
b.) *Magic Carpet 'Round the World*

Did You Know?

SPACE MOUNTAIN, CONSTRUCTED AFTER THE *WDW RAILROAD*, IS THE ONLY ATTRACTION IN THE MAGIC KINGDOM TO BE LOCATED OUTSIDE THE PERIMETER OF ITS TRACK.

c.) *The American Adventure*
d.) *The Hall of Presidents*

143. Approximately how fast do the rockets on the *Space Mountain* roller coaster go?
a.) 15 mph
b.) 28 mph
c.) 55 mph
d.) "Faster than the speed of light"

144. Nine-Eye, the flying robot camera in *The Timekeeper*, was from ___?
a.) Mars
b.) "The Future"
c.) Cleveland
d.) Tomorrowland

145. *If You Had Wings* opened with what sponsor?
a.) Delta Airlines
b.) American Airlines
c.) Eastern Airlines
d.) United Airlines

146. Who is the voice of Cousin Orville in *Carousel of Progress*?
a.) Walt Disney
b.) Roy Disney
c.) Frank Sinatra
d.) Mel Blanc

147. In *Buzz Lightyear's Space Ranger Spin*, where must you travel on your Secret Mission?
a.) Sector 9
b.) Delta Quadrant
c.) Beyond the Sun
d.) Mutara Nebula

THE ANSWERS
TO CHAPTER TWO

1. b.) October 25, 1971
After Walt Disney's untimely death in 1966, his brother, Roy O. Disney, took hold of the WDW project to see his brother's dreams fulfilled. On October 25, 1971, Roy dedicated the park to Walt's memory. Standing in Town Square with Walt's most famous creation, Mickey Mouse, Roy read the dedication plaque that stands today under the flagpole:

"WALT DISNEY WORLD is a tribute to the philosophy and life of Walter Elias Disney . . . and to the talents, the dedication, and the loyalty of the entire Disney organization that made Walt Disney's dream come true. May Walt Disney World bring Joy and Inspiration and New Knowledge to all who come to this happy place . . . a Magic Kingdom where the young at heart of all ages can laugh and play and learn together. Dedicated this 25th day of October, 1971." Less than two months later, on December 20, 1971, Roy passed away.

2. a.) *Snow White's Scary Adventures*
Snow White's Scary Adventures is based on Disney's 1937 classic, *Snow White and the Seven Dwarfs*, the world's first full-length animated film. True to the original, the attraction takes you on a three-minute trip through scenes from the Grimms' fairy tale and includes appearances by the Wicked Witch and all seven dwarfs.

3. b.) *If You Had Wings*
The late Thurl Ravenscroft, the famous voice behind Tony the Tiger, sings lead on the "Grim Grinning Ghosts" song in *The Haunted Mansion*. He is also the voice of Fritz in the *Enchanted Tiki Room*, Buff the Buffalo in the *Country Bear Jamboree*, and several characters in *Pirates of the Caribbean*. He even provided the narration for the *Disneyland Railroad* steam trains at one time. Thurl passed away in 2005.

4. d.) 750 feet
Since July 4, 1985, Tinker Bell has launched the nightly fireworks displays by flying from Cinderella Castle to Tomorrowland. She "flies" (in a special flying harness, often referred to as a "Peter Pan rig") at about 15 mph for 34 seconds during her 750-foot trip. During periods of high wind and inclement weather, Tink (who weighs somewhere in the

neighborhood of 90 pounds) takes the night off.

5. c.) *Liberty Square Riverboat*

The first "new" attraction to open after WDW's Grand Opening on October 1, 1971, was the *Liberty Square Riverboat*, which took its maiden voyage on October 2, 1971. *Peter Pan's Flight* was the second "new" attraction. It opened the next day, October 3, 1971.

6. a.) **Fantasyland**

Lancer's Inn was a quick-service restaurant that served pizza and snacks from 1971 until 1986, when it was replaced by Gurgi's Munchies & Crunchies. (Gurgi was a character in Disney's animated feature *The Black Cauldron*). In 1993, the eatery became Lumiere's Kitchen, which was replaced by Village Fry Shoppe in 2006.

7. b.) **Ward Kimball**

Ward Kimball was one of Disney's top animators. He joined the company in 1934 and, among his many achievements, created the character of "Jiminy Cricket" for *Pinocchio*. *WDW Railroad*'s #5 locomotive was named for him and dedicated in his presence in 1997. The *Ward Kimball* engine was a 2-4-4 Forney-type, made by Davenport Locomotive Works in 1927. It was actually acquired for Disneyland (not WDW) in a trade with southern California railroad enthusiast Bill Norred. When it proved too big for the California park, it was sent to Florida. Ironically, it was underpowered for the slight incline near WDW's Toontown Fair station. It was briefly displayed in Epcot during Black History Month in 1996, but eventually, it was traded for a Forney

locomotive that became Disneyland's #5 *Ward Kimball* engine.

8. d.) *SpectroMagic*

"Ladies and gentlemen, boys and girls, Walt Disney World proudly presents our spectacular festival pageant of nighttime magic and imagination in thousands of sparkling lights and electrosynthomagnetic musical sounds . . . the *Main Street Electrical Parade*." Floats in this legendary parade, which debuted in WDW on June 11, 1977, included the Blue Fairy (from *Pinocchio*), a tribute to America, and the Casey Junior Circus Train (from *Dumbo*) with Goofy at the controls, pulling a huge bass drum that read, "The Magic Kingdom Presents Main Street Electrical Parade" in multicolored lights. Fittingly, the parade's sponsor was Energizer because the lights, audio, and floats were powered by more than 27 tons of batteries — providing enough current to light 32 homes. After 15 seasons in Orlando, WDW's *Main Street Electrical Parade* made its final run down Main Street on September 14, 1991, and then headed for Disneyland Paris, where it opened in 1992 and still runs today. However, that wasn't quite the end of the parade in WDW. On May 28, 1999, after a dramatic "makeover" that included the addition of 575,000 new lights, Disneyland's slightly different version of the *Main Street Electrical

Parade opened in WDW as part of Disney's Millennium Celebration. It ended its WDW run permanently on April 1, 2001, but kept right on going — moving to Disney's California Adventure park and changing its name to *Disney's Electrical Parade*. It was replaced in WDW in both 1992 and 2001 by the *SpectroMagic* parade.

9. a.) *Mickey Mouse Revue*

Mickey Mouse Revue was an Opening Day E-ticket attraction. The fun, musical Audio-Animatronics show ran in Fantasyland from October 1, 1971, to September 14, 1980, before being taken down and sent to Tokyo Disneyland. It opened in Tokyo in April 1983 in almost its original format, giving it the distinction of being the first major Magic Kingdom attraction to be moved from the park. The *Mickey Mouse Revue* was directly inspired by Walt Disney, who had plans for an Audio-Animatronics show that would feature all of the Disney characters. The *Revue* included 73 characters portrayed by 81 Audio-Animatronics figures. Today, the theater where it played is home to *Mickey's Philharmagic*, a 3-D show similar in concept to the original *Mickey Mouse Revue*.

10. c.) D

The graceful *Plaza Swan Boats* operated seasonally from May 1973 to

August 1983 in the canal surrounding Cinderella Castle and through parts of Adventureland. Your guide for the 17-minute ride was usually a young, female Cast Member who pointed out numerous sights of interest as you floated by. The fleet included a dozen 26-passenger boats with names like *Tinker Belle*, *Flora*, and *Fauna* — including one that was used solely to clean the canals. They were powered by natural gas and used a water-jet propulsion system. Unlike many WDW boats, the *Plaza Swan Boats* were steered manually because their electronic guidance systems never worked correctly. Disney sold the boats long ago, but the green-roofed dock on the water's edge between Cinderella Castle and Tomorrowland still stands.

11. b.) Frontierland
You can reach Frontierland only by

Did You Know?

IN *SPACE MOUNTAIN* THERE ARE TWO SEPARATE RIDE TRACKS. ALPHA, THE LEFT TRACK, IS 3,196 FEET LONG, WHILE THE RIGHT TRACK, OMEGA, IS 3,186 FEET. ALPHA IS LONGER BECAUSE IT CROSSES OVER OMEGA AT ONE POINT.

passing through Liberty Square or Adventureland. Similarly, you can reach Mickey's Toontown Fair only by walking through Fantasyland or Tomorrowland (or via the *WDW Railroad*). All of the other lands in the MK have their own "spoke" off the central hub.

12. d.) *WDW Railroad*

When Walt Disney, an avid railroad fan, built Disneyland, he constructed the *Santa Fe & Disneyland Railroad* (with the help of the Santa Fe Railroad company), a 5/8-scale live steam train that circled the park. He wanted his Florida theme park to include steam trains, too. In 1969, Disney Imagineers traveled to Mexi-co to look for locomotives that could be refurbished and used to transport Guests. They purchased four from the United Railways of Yucatan. The engines were transported to Florida, where, in just two years, they were magically transformed into Victori-an-era locomotives grand enough to bear the Walt Disney name. In fact, the *WDW Railroad* was the first at-traction to be completed for WDW.

13. b.) Smoke Tree Ranch

So, what did Walt Disney, the man who single-handedly invented the theme park, do for fun? He'd go to Palm Springs, California, that's what. Walt and his wife bought their first Palm Springs home in 1948 at the

upscale Smoke Tree Ranch. The resort was very private — members only — and you had to be recommended by a committee to become a member. When Walt petitioned to join the community, many on the board did not want the "Hollywood lifestyle" invading their quiet retreat. So to prove his interest in the community, Walt had his Imagineers design and construct three cottages on the Ranch, prompting approval by the committee. These "Disney Cottages" still stand today, as does "Walt Disney Hall," a meeting and banquet facility next to the pool and not far from one of Walt's favorite bowling greens. At Smoke Tree Ranch, Walt was known to ride horseback, lawn bowl, and try to interest some of his neighbors to invest in his crazy idea for an amusement park. He often wore a tie clip emblazoned with an "STR" emblem.

14. d.) Main Street, U.S.A.

There is a Chinese restaurant on Main Street . . . Well, not really. Look at the second floor window above Casey's Corner and you'll see a sign for a Chinese Restaurant, serving Fine Foods and Imported Teas. "Jim Armstrong – Vegetable Buyer" is written below this pane, honoring a former Cast Member from the food services division.

15. a.) Cindy Williams

Cindy Williams (yes, from *Laverne and Shirley*) cut the ribbon for the June 18, 1988, grand opening of Mickey's Birthdayland, which was also attended by First Lady Nancy Reagan.

16. c.) *Admiral Joe Fowler*

The *Admiral Joe Fowler* took its first trip around the Rivers of America on October 2, 1971 — just one day after WDW opened. A D-ticket attraction, the boat was named for the retired U.S. Navy admiral who was responsible for overseeing the construction of both Disneyland and WDW. Unfortunately, the boat was dropped from a crane and sustained irreparable hull damage during routine maintenance in dry dock in 1980, forcing it into early retirement.

17. a.) 5

Each of the 4 *WDWRR* trains has 5 cars and can hold approximately 360 Guests and 2 wheelchairs.

18. b.) Jiminy Cricket

Wishes is a nighttime spectacular that combines magical moments from Disney films with spectacular pyrotechnic effects. It is many times the size of its predecessor, the *Fantasy in the Sky* fireworks show (which had run for 27 years before *Wishes* replaced it in October 2003). In fact, *Wishes* is the largest pyrotechnic display ever staged in the MK. Narrator Jiminy Cricket (aka Pinocchio's conscience) takes us through a story about making wishes come true: "I bet a lot of you folks don't believe that — about a wish coming true, do ya? Well, I didn't either. Of course, I'm just a cricket, but let me tell ya what changed my mind. Ya see, the most fantastic, magical things can happen — and it all starts with a wish!"

19. c.) *Grand Prix Raceway*
The track for the *Grand Prix Raceway* (now known as the *Tomorrowland Indy Speedway*) was shortened and moved slightly in 1988 to allow for construction for Mickey's Birthdayland.

20. d.) *Cinderella's Golden Carrousel*
The carousel was built in 1917 by the Philadelphia Toboggan Company for use in Palace Garden in Detroit, Michigan, where it was known as the "Liberty" carousel, suggestive of the nation's post-war, patriotic sentiments. It was moved to Olympic Park in Maplewood, New Jersey, after a refurbishment in 1928. Disney Imagineers found it there in 1967 and restored it for use at WDW.

21. d.) 100,000
The Magic Kingdom can hold 100,000 Guests. However, Disney often closes the MK parking lots when 75,000 Guests have gone through the turnstiles because it has to allow room for its resort hotel Guests, who continue to arrive by WDW transport (buses and monorails) after the lots are closed.

22. c.) *Roy O. Disney*
The whistle on the *Roy O. Disney*, WDW Engine 4, was salvaged from the *Admiral Joe Fowler* riverboat after it was destroyed in dry dock in 1980. It sounds much lower than the whistles of the other three *WDWRR* locomotives.

23. d.) Avenue of the Planets
The Avenue of the Planets joins the Magic Kingdom's central hub to Tomorrowland's Rockettower Plaza, where Guests can arrange transportation on the *Tomorrowland Transit Authority*, visit the Tomorrowland Interplanetary Convention Center, and watch *Walt Disney's Carousel of Progress* (sponsored by the Tomorrowland Metro-Retro Society).

24. c.) Mr. Toad
During the concept stages prior to construction, a number of very different rides were planned that never made it into the park. For example, Fantasyland was going to have several different "dark rides." They included a Sleeping Beauty ride (instead of a Snow White attraction), a "Jolly Holiday with Mary Poppins" ride (in place of *Peter Pan's Flight*),

and an Ichabod Crane "Headless Horseman" ride. *Mr. Toad's Wild Ride* was not among the original concepts.

25. b.) Orson Welles
The voice of famed actor and director Orson Welles could be heard in the *If You Had Wings* queue area.

26. d.) *Skyway*
Operational on Opening Day, the *Skyway* was a five-minute cable-car style ride that ran between Fantasyland and Tomorrowland, passing over the *Cinderella's Golden Carrousel* tent and the *Grand Prix Raceway. 20,000 Leagues Under the Sea* opened on October 14, 1971; *If You Had Wings* on June 5, 1972. The *Carousel of Progress* left Disneyland in 1973 but didn't open in WDW until January 15, 1975.

27. a.) Refreshment Corner
On May 27, 1995, the best place to get a hot dog in all of WDW changed its name from Refreshment Corner to Casey's Corner, complete with nostalgic baseball theme (a la Casey at the bat).

28. b.) 108 feet
According to a sign at the Main Street Railroad Station, the Magic Kingdom's elevation is 108 feet.

29. c.) Kodak
The 15-minute daytime *Share a*

Dream Come True parade runs from Frontierland to Main Street, U.S.A. This parade of giant snow globes, presented by Kodak, is a tribute to classic Disney characters and stories.

30. a.) *The Diamond Horseshoe Revue*
This variety show set in the Old West opened with the MK in 1971 and used to play throughout the day. Although the show was free and didn't require a ticket, it normally required reservations because the theater served meals before the show. The review's name was changed to the *Diamond Horseshoe Jamboree* on October 1, 1986. Reservations were no longer required as of April 7,

1995, when the name changed yet again — to the *Diamond Horseshoe Saloon Revue* — and the sit-down meal menu gave way to sandwiches and drinks (like the great root beer!). The Saloon shared a kitchen with the Adventureland Verandah (located behind the show building).

31. c.) Rivers of America
The Rivers of America surrounds Tom Sawyer Island and is home to the *Liberty Belle* riverboat (formerly known as the *Richard F. Irvine*). Until the mid 1990s, Guests could travel on the *Gullywhumper* or the *Bertha Mae* if they took a ride on one of Mike Fink's keelboats.

32. a.) 10 mph
The four narrow-gauge steam trains that make up the *WDW Railroad* fleet take you on a relaxing journey around the park. The steam engines, built between 1916 and 1928, travel at a speed of about 10 miles per hour. The passenger cars were built between 1970 and 1971.

33. d.) *Peter Pan's Flight*
When the MK first opened in 1971, ticket coupons were used to gain admission to individual attractions. They ranged from A through E, with E tickets required for the very best rides. The first E-ticket attractions were the *Jungle Cruise, Country Bear Jamboree, Hall of Presidents, The Haunted Mansion, "it's a small world,"* and *20,000 Leagues Under the Sea.*

34. d.) 1999
The *Skyway*, a one-way D-ticket ride between Fantasyland and Tomorrowland, closed for good on November 10, 1999. Why? Well, despite rumors that it closed for safety reasons after a Guest fell from a ride car, the *Skyway* closed for more practical reasons: It was unprofitable, very slow loading, and it was extremely difficult to accommodate Guests with disabilities on it. A wheelchair-bound Guest had to leave the chair on the loading area and take a round-trip ride. However, reports that there was a death on the *Skyway* are in fact true, although it was not a Guest who died. In February 1999, a part-time Cast Member, who wasn't wearing protective equipment or a safety harness, accidentally fell to his death while working in the loading area.

35. a.) Cast Members
On July 18th, 2005, the entire WDW Cast was honored with a window on Main Street, U.S.A. It reads "Magic Kingdom Casting Agency – It Takes People to Make the Dream a Reality." You'll find it on a building next to the Main Street Athletic Club.

36. b.) *SpectroMagic*
The MK's most technologically ad-

vanced parade to date, *SpectroMagic* features classic Disney characters like Mickey (who conjures up the parade through his sparkling crystal ball) and Goofy (who performs in the parade band). *SpectroMagic* uses advanced technologies, such as 100 miles of fiber-optic cables and threads, to cast more than 72,000 watts of light onto the park's streets. The more than 250,000 fiber-optic points of light form dancing Disney characters, birds, butterflies, and various animals. More than 30 computers are used to control the lights alone! The parade's opening features Mickey and the Spectrowizards, while the finale includes the wicked Chernabog from *Fantasia*.

37. d.) 3,000,000

Want to find out how the four

WDWRR locomotives are operated and maintained to accommodate more than 3,000,000 passengers every year? Disney's "Magic Behind Our Steam Trains" guided tour takes Guests to the "roundhouse," where engineers discuss the railroad's history and operations. Guests taking

the tour used to be given an actual spike from the railroad as a souvenir, but since the 9/11 tragedy they've been given a collector's pin instead because the spikes were often confiscated at the airport.

Main Street, U.S.A.

38. a.) Marceline, Missouri

Main Street, U.S.A. is loosely based on the town of Marceline, Missouri, circa 1910, when it was home to about 5,000 people. Located in north central Missouri, about 120 miles northeast of Kansas City, Marceline sprang up along the route of the Atchison, Topeka and Santa Fe Railroad in 1888. By April 1906, when the Disney family settled nearby on a 45-acre farm, the town was a stop for railroad crew changes and refueling. Walt was just four years old at the time and he quickly became interested in trains. He enjoyed walking to the railroad tracks to watch the trains come in and out of the station, and his Uncle Martin, a train conductor, frequently stayed with the Disneys when he was in town. Although his family sold the farm and moved to Kansas City in 1910, Walt spoke fondly of Marceline throughout his life, and his memories of it inspired his idealistic Main Street, U.S.A. In 1956, the

town named a new swimming pool and recreation center after its most famous son, which prompted Walt's return to his boyhood home with his brother Roy. Four years later, on October 13, 1960, the "Walt Disney Elementary School" opened. Walt came to the dedication ceremony by train; it was the first time the Santa Fe Super Chief had ever stopped in Marceline.

39. b.) 2
Main Street, U.S.A. is just two blocks long, stretching from Town Square, in front of the *WDW Railroad* Station, up to the Central Plaza hub.

40. d.) Omnibus
When the Magic Kingdom opened in 1971, you could take a double-decker bus, called an Omnibus, on a one-way trip down Main Street. The buses were later moved to EPCOT Center to transport Guests around the World Showcase Lagoon.

41. c.) House of Magic
A great loss to the Magic Kingdom, the House of Magic sold magic tricks and monster masks, as well as tons of books and inexpensive gags. Sadly, the House of Magic, the Main Street Bookstore, and the Penny Arcade all closed on March 19, 1995. They were replaced by a single store, the Main Street Athletic Shop, in the summer of '95.

42. b.) George Weaver
Feel free to go up and shake hands with Mayor George Weaver. He's running for reelection, so you'll see him on Main Street throughout the day. Other town characters you may run into include town gossip Tabitha Quidnunk, socialite Hildegard Olivia Harding, and *Main Street Gazette* reporter and Disney "Pin-thusiast" Scoop Sanderson (who gives Pin Talks at Exposition Hall daily Wednesday through Sunday). Cast Members playing these char-

acters are happy to interact with Guests; just be sure to address them as the characters they are playing.

43. a.) Gulf Oil
Gulf sponsored the Hospitality House restaurant and the *Walt Disney Story* attraction from 1973 until about 1979. Those defunct entities once occupied the building now known as the Town Square Exposition Hall (currently home to a camera center, some exhibits, and a small theater showing classic Disney cartoons).

44. d.) *Sharing the Magic*
This statue of Roy O. Disney and Minnie Mouse sitting on a bench together was created by Disney Legend and leading sculptor Blaine Gibson, who is one of five Walt Disney Imagineering premier artists honored together with a window on Main Street, U.S.A. That window reads: "Center Street Academy of Fine Art Painting & Sculpture: Collin Campbell, Blaine Gibson,

Herb Ryman, Mary Blair, Dorothea Redmond." *Sharing the Magic* was placed in Town Square in October 1999 and dedicated on October 25, 1999 – precisely 28 years to the day after Roy O. Disney dedicated the Magic Kingdom.

45. c.) Station Break
Guest lockers used to be located at "Station Break" underneath the Main Street Train Station, along with the package pick-up desk for items purchased at the park's shops. You can still pick up items there, but the lockers are now outside the station.

46. b.) The Dapper Dans
The Dapper Dans quartet began singing in Disneyland in 1959, where they continue to perform to this day. In 1971, a second Dapper Dans quartet was formed to perform in WDW. They can be heard throughout the day on Main Street, U.S.A., as well as near the barbershop (of course).

Did You Know?

YOU CAN LISTEN IN ON AN OLD "PARTY LINE" PHONE CONVERSATION WHEN YOU VISIT MAIN STREET, U.S.A. AS YOU ENTER THE MK, HEAD DOWN THE FIRST ALLEY ON THE RIGHT SIDE OF THE STREET. NEXT TO THE REGISTER IN THE MARKET HOUSE CORNER STORE, PICK UP THE PHONE AND LISTEN IN!

47. b.) 13

Main Street, U.S.A. is a great place to find everything from delicious pastries, to sweet treats, to Character Meals, to the best darn hot dog in WDW. Check out such eateries as Casey's Corner, The Crystal Palace, Main Street Bakery, Plaza Ice Cream Parlor, The Plaza Restaurant, and of course, Tony's Town Square.

48. d.) Main Street Candy Station

Shops have come and gone on Main Street, U.S.A. over the years — including one or two you'd never expect to have seen there at all! Among those now gone are the Holiday Corner (which sold Christmas accessories and candles), the Wonderland of Wax candle shop, and the Main

Street Book Store (which also sold writing accessories and greeting cards). Surprisingly, there was also a Tobacconist shop that sold pipes and various kinds of tobacco. Why surprising? Because Walt Disney died in 1966 of lung cancer attributed to years of cigarette smoking.

49. c.) Plaza Ice Cream Parlor

When the Magic Kingdom was created, Walt Disney wanted his Guests to feel as though they were part of a movie come to life, and there are numerous touches all along Main Street, U.S.A. that illustrate that metaphor. Like all movies, the Magic Kingdom had to have its opening and closing credits. This is accomplished by placing the names of

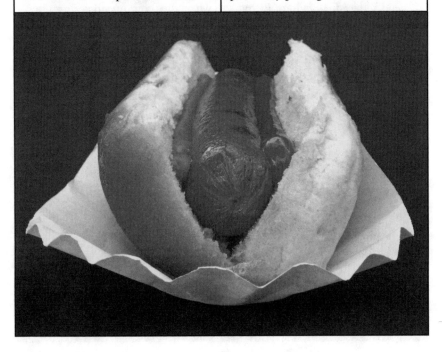

Did You Know?

ONLY ONE BUILDING ON MAIN STREET, U.S.A.
IS BUILT TO FULL SCALE, EXPOSITION HALL. THIS
WAS DONE TO HIDE THE CONTEMPORARY RESORT.
SEEING IT WOULD HAVE RUINED THE ILLUSION
THAT YOU ARE WALKING DOWN THE STREET OF
A NINETEENTH CENTURY TOWN.

people who were important to the creation of WDW on the windows over the shops on Main Street, U.S.A. As you walk into the park, the windows are the opening credits, and they become the closing credits as you exit. Walt Disney's "credit" is the first one you see on both the way in and out. His name appears on a window above the railroad station at the entrance to the park (his "opening credit") and in another window over the Plaza Ice Cream Parlor facing the Castle, making "Walter E. Disney" the first name you see in the "closing credits," too.

Adventureland

50. b.) 1805
The full sign outside this wonderful, walk-through attraction reads:
"On this site, July 17, 1805, the Swiss Family Robinson, composed of myself, my good wife, my three sons Fritz, Ernst and little Francis,

were the sole survivors by the grace of God, of the ill-fated ship, SWALLOW. From the wreckage we built our home in this tree for protection on this uncharted shore. – *Franz*"

51. c.) 3
Just three Adventureland attractions were operational on Opening Day: the *Swiss Family Treehouse, Jungle Cruise*, and the *Tropical Serenade* (later rehabbed and reopened as *The Enchanted Tiki Room – Under New Management*). These attractions have stayed close to their original format over the years as numerous other attractions and shops were added.

52. c.) Live animals
It has long been rumored that Walt Disney wanted to use live animals throughout the *Jungle Cruise*. The idea was dropped when the Imagineers realized that not only would they not be able to keep the animals in the locations where they wanted them, but also that many

animals would be asleep in the middle of the day, when the temperature is at its highest.

53. d.) Cat
A black cat is featured on the white stripe between the two red stripes on the Swiss Family Robinson crest. You can see the crest at the attraction's entrance.

54. b.) Uhoa
Uhoa is the Tiki God of Disaster. Remember, when you mess with Polynesia, the Tiki Gods will seize ya!

55. a.) *The Enchanted Tiki Room*
Walt Disney was inspired to create *The Enchanted Tiki Room* by a fascinating antique animated bird he found in a New Orleans shop. The attraction was conceived as a dinner show, but the concept proved impractical. Wally Boag and Fulton Burley wrote the script for the original *Tiki Room* show, which opened in Disneyland in 1963.

56. b.) 10 minutes
The WDW version of *Pirates of the Caribbean* is a little bit shorter than the one in Disneyland, which has a

longer drop and additional scenes.

57. d.) Natural gas
Compressed natural gas is used to power the *Jungle Cruise* boats because it is clean burning and environmentally friendly.

58. a.) *The Enchanted Tiki Room*
WDW's *Tropical Serenade* opened with the Magic Kingdom in 1971 and was based on Disneyland's popular *Enchanted Tiki Room* attraction, which opened in 1963. It was in the Disneyland version that Guests were entertained by the first Audio-Animatronics performers. *Tropical Serenade* closed for a major rehab in 1997 and reopened as *The Enchant-*

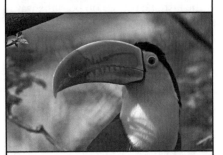

ed Tiki Room – Under New Management on April 5, 1998, featuring several new musical numbers along

Did You Know?

THE WDW VERSION OF *PIRATES OF THE CARIBBEAN* IS SHORTER THAN THE DISNEYLAND VERSION.

with the original cast of characters (including the show's original four hosts, José, Michael, Pierre, and Fritz) and the new "owners" of the Tiki Room, Iago and Zazu.

59. c.) Artemus

When WDW's *Enchanted Tiki Room* first opened (as the *Tropical Serenade*), it was sponsored by and closely tied to the Florida Citrus Growers Association. For more than 21 years, a "barker bird" perched outside the funny, upbeat attraction and sang for passing Guests, begging them to come into the Tiki Room. In 1992, Artemus, a blue toucan with a Caribbean accent, took over. He lasted until 1997, when the *Tropical Serenade* closed for a major rehab.

60. b.) Disneyodendron

There are only four of these Disney-created "trees" in the world — the others are in Anaheim, Tokyo, and Paris. The WDW *Swiss Family Treehouse* is located in a *Disneyodendron eximus*, which translates into "out of the ordinary Disney tree." Disneyland's attraction is in a *Disneyodendron semperflorens grandis*, which means "large, always blooming Disney tree." The trees and attractions in all four parks were inspired by the 1960 Disney film, *The Swiss Family Robinson*.

61. a.) Mekong

During your perilous and often hilarious *Jungle Cruise* expedition, you travel through numerous continents

and ply four notable rivers. In order, you make your way through South America on the Amazon, central Africa on the Congo, Egypt on the Nile (where you see the "backside of water"), and finally through Southeast Asia on the Mekong river. (Worried that your comedic skipper is spending too much time on jokes and not enough time navigating the dangerous rivers? Don't. The boats on the *Jungle Cruise* have wheels on the bottom that are fitted into a guided rail system. Therefore the skippers don't have to worry about steering, they just do it for effect. They can, however, control the forward and reverse speed of the boat.)

62. d.) The ships' names differed. The Johann David Wyss novel, *The Swiss Family Robinson*, published in 1812, gave no name to the doomed vessel. Disney, on the other hand, has given it several different names. In WDW, it is called the *Swallow*. In Disneyland, the sign referred to the ship as the *Recovery* when the *Swiss Family Treehouse* first opened,

but the vessel's name was changed to *Titus* later on during a rehab. The only name given in the novel was to the house itself, which the author called Falconhurst.

Frontierland

63. a.) Jack Dalton You'll find Marshall Dalton keepin' the peace in Frontierland at various times throughout the day. He and such Wild West characters as Prospector "Gold Dust Gus" seamlessly blend into the theme of the land. The Cast Members playing them will gladly interact with Guests in on-the-spot improvisations.

Did You Know?

NICK STEWART, THE VOICE OF THE ORIGINAL BRER BEAR IN THE *SONG OF THE SOUTH* FILM, ALSO PROVIDED THE VOICE FOR *SPLASH MOUNTAIN*'S BRER BEAR.

64. d.) Fred

Legendary Disney Imagineer Marc Davis created the original character designs for this classic attraction. In the show's opening song, "The Bear Band Serenade," we learn that big Fred's playin' the mouth harp and he plays it kinda sad. According to Fred's wife, he's kinda lazy and a tune is the ONLY thing he can carry!

65. c.) 5 stories

One of WDW's most popular attractions, *Splash Mountain* opened in 1992. It takes Guests on an 11-minute journey that's topped off by a 40 mph, 52.5-foot (5-story) final drop into the Briar Patch. In addition to its 68 Audio-Animatronics, *Splash Mountain* has the largest animated prop in any Disney park: the *Zip-A-Dee Lady* showboat is 36 feet long and 22 feet high!

66. d.) "Dried out"

The previous numbers are crossed out on the population sign for the town through which the *Big Thunder Mountain Railroad* runs, leaving just "dried out" as the current number of residents. The sign, which can only be seen while riding on the *WDW Railroad,* is right above the man in the red long johns who is taking a bath in the floating tub.

67. a.) Aunt Polly's Dockside Inn

Serving only snacks and beverages, Aunt Polly's Dockside Inn, open seasonally, is located on Tom Sawyer Island, on the banks of the Rivers of America. It is a nice place to sit in the shade (aaahhhhhh . . .) and have a peanut butter and jelly sandwich or an ice cream sundae, while watching the *Liberty Belle* riverboat make its way around the island.

68. b.) Henry

The 15-minute Audio-Animatronics show is hosted by Henry, who introduces and sings songs with some of the other hilarious, yet quite talented, country bears.

69. b.) Tumbleweed

"The tiny town of Tumbleweed" is mentioned on the *WDW Railroad* as you pass by Big Thunder Mountain and through the deserted mining town.

70. c.) 1973

The relaxing walk-through attraction *Tom Sawyer Island* opened almost two years after the Magic Kingdom, in 1973.

71. b.) Tennessee

The first chorus of the *Country Bear* theme song introduces Tennessee, who is one of the singers in The Five Bear Rugs:

"The Bear Band bears will play now
In the good ol' key of G.
Zeek and Zed and Ted and Fred
And a bear named Tennessee."

72. a.) Flash flood

Unlike the Disneyland version of *Big Thunder Mountain Railroad*, the WDW version is slightly longer, thanks to the addition of a scene that shows the remains of the tiny mining town that was destroyed by a flash flood.

73. b.) "Blood on the Saddle"

Big Al looks about as depressed as he does large as he belts out his signature song, "Blood on the Saddle." Big Al was voiced by legendary country music star Tex Ritter, and "Blood on the Saddle" is also the name of a CD collection of Ritter's recordings made from 1932 to 1947. "My Woman Ain't Pretty, But She Don't Swear None" is performed by Liver Lips McGrowl. "The Ballad of Davy Crockett" is performed by Henry, and "He's Big Around the Middle and He's Broad Across the Rump" is performed by almost all the other bears, who are trying to drown out Big Al's singing!

74. b.) *Song of the South*

Frontierland's *Splash Mountain* is based on the animated sequences of the 1946 Walt Disney Academy-Award winning classic, *Song of the South*. The film won two Academy Awards: "Zip-A-Dee-Doo-Dah" won the Oscar for Best Song, and James Baskett was awarded an honorary Oscar for his portrayal of Uncle Remus, "friend and story-teller to the children of the world." The film was also nominated for Best Scoring of a Musical Picture.

75. d.) Sam Clemens

The three wooden rafts that take you to Tom Sawyer Island are named after characters in the book, *The Adventures of Tom Sawyer* — Tom Sawyer, Injun Joe, and Becky Thatcher. Each raft has a maximum capacity of about 70 people. These rafts aren't as "low-tech" as 'most everything else on the island. Although the rafts look like they are constructed of logs, they are actually made of fiberglass and steel and are powered by environmentally friendly natural gas engines. The only wood on them is decorative.

76. c.) 30

There are five cars per train, with six Guests per car. Thus, 30 Guests may ride the *BTMRR* at one time.

77. b.) The Zip-A-Dee-Doo-Dah River Run

Splash Mountain premiered in Disneyland in 1989, before opening in WDW just three years later. It was the brainchild of Imagineer Tony Baxter. During his morning commute to work, he came up with the idea of an attraction that could cool off guests and bring them into Disneyland's Bear Country. It would use Audio-Animatronics figures from the recently closed *America Sings* attraction and be themed to the Disney film *Song of the South.* Like many attractions, this one had several working titles during its development, including "The Zip-A-Dee-Doo-Dah River Run" and "The Song of the South Log Flume Ride."

78. c.) Fort Sam Clemens

Sam Clemens was American author Mark Twain's real name. Fort Sam Clemens, Injun Joe's Cave, and the Mystery Mine were just a few of the surprises you would find along the way when you visited Tom Sawyer Island in earlier days. In 1996, though, the fort's name was changed to Fort Langhorn to coincide with the release of the live-action Disney film, *Tom and Huck*, which is based on the Mark Twain novels about those legendary boyhood friends.

79. a.) *Western River Expedition*

By 1968, design work had begun for a boat ride in Frontierland that would transport Guests into the days of cowboys and Indians, past scenes of animals in natural settings, dance hall girls, bank robbers, Indians, and other frontier sights. Although the concept sketches for it were featured on postcards and park guide maps, it remains one of Disney's most famous unbuilt attractions. In the original concept, the *Western River Expedition* would have been a musical *Pirates of the Caribbean*-style ride located deep inside the Thunder Mesa mountain range and would have been just one of three planned Thunder Mesa attractions. The *Big Thunder Mountain Railroad* is a spin-off of the Thunder Mesa concept — the only part of it that made it into the park.

Liberty Square

80. b.) Lucretia

You'll find the names of Bluebeard's seven wives on a memorial as you exit *The Haunted Mansion.* They are Lucretia, who "did him in" in 1440, and her predecessors: Penelope, Abigail, Anastasia, Prudence, Phoebe, and Eugenia. The six were laid to rest between 1434 and 1439.

81. b.) The Sons and Daughters of Liberty

In the 1970s, a daily ceremony was held in Liberty Square in front of the Liberty Bell. Called "The Sons and Daughters of Liberty," the ceremony (which no longer takes place) involved a fife and drum corps marching with Cast Members, all clad in Revolutionary-era costuming. A Cast Member would choose a boy and girl from the crowd to be the official "son and daughter" of Liberty.

82. d.) Fred

"Here lies
good old Fred,
A great big rock
fell on his head
R.I.P."

The inscription on Fred's gravestone is a tribute to Disney Legend, Fred Joerger, an art director who created

numerous plaster effects for *The Haunted Mansion*. He is also honored in a window above Main Street, U.S.A.

83. a.) *One Nation Under God*

Walt Disney originally had planned to build a Liberty Square land in Disneyland. *One Nation Under God* was a proposed attraction for it that was to feature Abraham Lincoln addressing all of the other U.S. presidents. When the president of the upcoming New York World's Fair visited the Disney Studios, he saw the plans for *One Nation Under God* and wanted it for the Fair. Since it couldn't be completed in time, an abridged version was shown, known as "Great Moments with Mr. Lincoln." Walt's *One Nation Under God* was to have been housed in a replica of Philadelphia's Independence Hall. It would have been located between Disneyland's Tomorrowland and Main Street, U.S.A. Although the attraction never materialized exactly as and where Walt conceived it, WDW's *Hall of Presidents* was created using his concepts.

84. b.) Gus, Ezra and Phineas

The little ghost with the ball and chain is Gus, while the tall, skinny skeleton is Ezra. Their hunched-over friend with the top hat is Phineas. According to (Cast Member) legend, Ezra Dobbins and Phineas Queeg

became friends of Gus Gracey when the three were cellmates at the Salem Asylum for the Criminally Insane. They escaped together, hitchhiking down the road. Sometime later, Madame Leota cast a spell banishing the ghost of Gus to the Mansion for eternity. However, she eventually took pity on him and summoned his old friends to keep him company, and so they continue to hitchhike to this day.

85. c.) Mark Twain

Take a leisurely 17-minute tour aboard the *Liberty Belle*, an authentic three-deck paddleboat. This slow-moving attraction is narrated by Mark Twain, whose charm and wit enhance the wonderful, often overlooked experience. Twain, who grew up on the banks of the

Mississippi River near Hannibal, Missouri, aspired to be a river pilot when he was a boy.

86. d.) Little Leota
The little ghost at the end of the ride who beckons you to "hurry back" is known as "Little Leota." The ghost is a small doll propped on the ledge of a crypt, dressed in a flowing wedding gown. Her talking face is actually projected onto the doll from a hidden projector. The face and voice of Little Leota is that of the late Leota Thomas (whose maiden name was, ironically, Toombs), a former Disney artist. The Imagineers asked her to stand-in just to test the effect but then decided to keep her performance in the final version of the attraction. (The face of Madame Leota, the character in the crystal ball, was also provided by Leota Thomas.)

87. c.) 1989
The Liberty Bell in WDW's Liberty Square was cast in 1989 from a mold taken directly from the real Liberty Bell in Philadelphia, making WDW's a "second generation" bell. It is the only one in existence; once the replica was cast, the mold taken from the original was destroyed.

88. b.) Master Gracey
"Master Gracey" is the "owner" of *The Haunted Mansion*. He was named after Imagineer Yale Gracey,

who was responsible for creating many of the incredible special effects for the attraction. Gracey joined Disney in 1939, working first as a layout artist on *Pinocchio* and then as Art Director for *Fantasia*. In 1961, he joined the WED Enterprises division of Disney and began creating special effects for several attractions, most notably the *Pirates of the Caribbean*. Gracey retired from Disney in 1975 and died in September 1983, at age 72. He is "remembered" with a tombstone in the Mansion's graveyard that reads: "Master Gracey laid to rest, no mourning please at his request, Farewell."

89. a.) A carpet containing the Presidential Seal
The Hall of Presidents in WDW is the only place in the world other than the White House that is

Did You Know?

LOOK CLOSELY AT THE FACADES OF THE BUILDINGS IN LIBERTY SQUARE. THEIR CHANGING STYLES MARK A PROGRESSION THROUGH TIME. IF YOU PUT AN "18" IN FRONT OF EACH HOUSE NUMBER, YOU'LL GET THE YEAR THE BUILDING'S FACADE WAS IN STYLE (E.G. 1826).

allowed to use a carpet with the Official Presidential Seal. You'll find the carpet in the rotunda.

90. c.) Paul Frees
The haunting voice of *The Haunted Mansion*'s narrator, the "Ghost Host," belongs to Paul Frees, a legendary voice actor. He has worked on a number of Disney projects, giving voice to numerous pirates from *Pirates of the Caribbean*, for example, and narrating Disneyland's *Great Moments with Mr. Lincoln* and *Adventure Thru Inner Space*. You may recognize his voice as that of Boris Badenov, from the animated cartoon series *The Bullwinkle Show*, as well as The Pillsbury Doughboy, Froot Loops cereal's Toucan Sam, and the narrator of the 1953 classic, *War of the Worlds*.

91. d.) Steam
The *Liberty Belle* riverboat is a real, working paddle steamer, built entirely from scratch in dry dock at WDW. Everything about the *Belle*

is authentic and working, except for the steering: the boat travels on a steel track hidden underwater!

92. a.) The Mello Men
"Grim Grinning Ghosts," the theme song for *The Haunted Mansion*, was written by Xavier Atencio (lyrics) and Buddy Baker (music) and recorded by the four-man singing group, the Mello Men. The four were Bill Lee, Max Smith, Bob Stevens, and Thurl Ravenscroft (probably the most famous). The broken singing bust in the *Mansion*'s graveyard scene has Thurl's face (although many have mistaken it for Walt Disney's). The Mello Men also sing "Yo Ho, (A Pirate's Life for Me)" in the *Pirates of the Caribbean* attraction and can be heard in a number of Disney film hits, such as "Painting the Roses Red" in *Alice in Wonderland*, "The Ballad of Davy Crockett," and as background dogs in "He's a Tramp" in *Lady and the Tramp*. In the 1960's, the Mello Men sang backup for none other than Elvis Presley.

Did You Know?

THE LIBERTY SQUARE CHRISTMAS SHOP IN THE MAGIC KINGDOM IS DESIGNED TO LOOK LIKE THREE SEPARATE SHOPS WITH THE WALLS BETWEEN THEM OPENED UP. THEY ARE SUPPOSED TO BE OWNED BY THREE DIFFERENT COLONIAL FAMILIES — A GERMAN FAMILY, A WOODCARVER'S FAMILY, AND A MUSICIAN'S FAMILY.

Fantasyland

93. c.) 26
Twenty-six classic Disney tunes play in the background of *Cinderella's Golden Carrousel*. The tunes, all but two from Disney animated films, are instrumentals played in calliope style. They include:

• "When You Wish Upon a Star," "Hi Diddle Dee Dee (An Actor's Life For Me)," and "Give a Little Whistle" from the film *Pinocchio*
• "So This Is Love," "The Work Song," and "A Dream Is a Wish Your Heart Makes" from *Cinderella*
• "Alice in Wonderland" from the film of the same name
• "Heigh Ho," "I'm Wishing," "Whistle While You Work," and "Someday My Prince Will Come" from *Snow White and the Seven Dwarfs*
• "Chim Chim Cheree" and "Feed The Birds (Tuppence a Bag)" from *Mary Poppins*

• "Be Our Guest" and "Gaston" from *Beauty and the Beast*
• "Colors of the Wind" from *Pocahontas*
• "Bella Notte" from *Lady and the Tramp*
• "A Whole New World" and "Prince Ali" from *Aladdin*
• "Once Upon a Dream" and "I Wonder" from *Sleeping Beauty*
• "Part of Your World" from *The Little Mermaid*
• "Second Star to the Right" and "You Can Fly! You Can Fly! You Can Fly!" from *Peter Pan*
• "Baby Mine" from *Dumbo*
• "Hakuna Matata" from *The Lion King*

94. d.) A mouse
The Dormouse pops his head out from the teapot during this madcap ride. Unlike the Disneyland version, the WDW *Mad Tea Party* has a canopy overhead to protect Guests from the elements.

Did You Know?

MADAME LEOTA'S VOICE WAS PERFORMED BY
ELEANOR AUDLEY. YOU MAY NOT KNOW THE NAME,
BUT IF YOU'VE EVER SEEN THE DISNEY ANIMATED
CLASSICS *SLEEPING BEAUTY* AND/OR *CINDERELLA*,
YOU WILL RECOGNIZE HER DISTINCTIVE VOICE AS
MALEFICENT AND LADY TREMAINE.

95. a.) Nowhere in Particular
Guests could (at one time) hop into one of J. Thaddeus Toad's motorcars and speed off to "Nowhere in Particular," in the wild ride based on the novel, *Wind in the Willows,* by Kenneth Grahame. "Nowhere in Particular" (aka "The Merrily Song") was also the name of the theme song that played throughout the attraction.

96. b.) A cowboy and an Indian
Of all the hundreds of figures of children in *"it's a small world,"* the United States is represented by only two, a cowboy and an Indian who appear in the final scene (the white room). (Just add a biker, a policeman, a construction worker, and a sailor and you have the Village People!)

97. b.) 10
During the refurbishment of *Dumbo the Flying Elephant* in 1993, the number of elephant ride vehicles was increased from 10 to 16. Also, the center cylinder topped by a mirrored ball was changed to include a hot-air balloon.

98. d.) "Rags to Riches"
The Cinderella fountain in Fantasyland is called "Rags to Riches." It was given this name partly because of the visual juxtaposition of a crown in a mural behind the fountain and the statue of a princess inside the fountain. As children look up from the fountain, the crown appears to be sitting on the princess's head.

99. a.) "Mickey Mouse Club March"
The orchestra is playing this famous song from the *Mickey Mouse Club* television show when Donald gets hold of Mickey's Sorcerer hat in *Mickey's PhilharMagic.*

100. c.) 5
The 87 horses on the *Carrousel* are arranged in five concentric circles,

each composed of a row of horses. Smaller "child friendly" horses are in the interior rows, with larger steeds on the outer rows.

101. d.) A mouse
Located on the spindle in the center of the circus ring that makes up the *Dumbo the Flying Elephant* ride is a hot air balloon. Perched atop the balloon is none other than Dumbo's friend, Timothy J. Mouse, who helped Dumbo discover his ability to fly using his oversized ears.

102. b.) UNICEF
"it's a small world – a Salute to UNICEF" was one of four attractions Disney presented at the New York World's Fair in 1964-65. However, Disney executives initially refused Pepsi-Cola's proposal that it build a Pepsi-sponsored UNICEF attraction for the Fair. When Walt heard about their decision, he overrode it. The attraction was designed by Imagineer Rolly Crump and built within a span of nine months. Imagineer Marc Davis designed the Audio-Animatronics children, and the overall look and feel of the ride was the work of legendary Disney Studios artist, Mary Blair. After the Fair closed, the entire attraction, with the exception of a large tower known as the "Tower of the Four Winds," was moved to Disneyland. A similar version was later built for WDW.

103. b.) 18
Inspired by Disney's 1951 animated interpretation of Lewis Carroll's *Alice in Wonderland*, the *Mad Tea Party* celebrates the Mad Hatter and March Hare's "Unbirthday" party. Take a minute-and-a-half ride in one of 18 whirling teacups that spin at your control on a giant "tea tray."

104. a.) Mexico
Of all the nations of the world represented in "*it's a small world,*" only one country's name is spelled out: Mexico. Can't find it? In the South America scene, look to the right side of the boat for a sombrero with the word "MEXICO" stitched into it.

105. b.) C
When WDW still used ticket books, *Mr. Toad* required a C ticket. The attraction was (unfortunately for some) replaced by *The Many Adventures of Winnie the Pooh* in 1999. Mr. Toad still rides on in Disneyland, but the ride there is different from the now-defunct Florida version.

Did You Know?

IT HAS LONG BEEN RUMORED THAT WALT DISNEY
(WHO PASSED AWAY BEFORE WDW OPENED)
NEVER RODE THE *DUMBO* ATTRACTION IN DISNEYLAND.
A STAUNCH DEMOCRAT, WALT BELIEVED THAT IF HE
WERE PHOTOGRAPHED IN AN ELEPHANT
(THE MASCOT OF THE REPUBLICAN PARTY),
IT COULD BE MISINTERPRETED BY THE MEDIA.

106. d.) Snow White was added to the attraction.
Where was she before the ride's 1994 refurbishment? That's what a lot of people asked as they exited the ride, having not seen the title character at all. The reason for this omission was that you, the Guest, were supposed to be playing the part of Snow White and experiencing her adventures, such as running from the witch and meeting the dwarfs. There were a number of other noticeable changes after the rehab: The Wicked Witch scenes were changed slightly to make them less scary for the kiddies; The ride cars were enlarged to accommodate more riders (the attraction had been notorious for its exceptionally long lines); Better Audio-Animatronics figures were installed; and the seven dwarfs were added to a few more scenes. The attraction initially changed in 1983, when the word "scary" was added to

the original name, *Snow White's Adventures*, to warn parents of small children who might be frightened by the dark ride.

Mickey's Toontown Fair

107. b.) Mickey's Birthdayland
Mickey's Toontown Fair was never meant to be. No, really. It was created in 1988 as "Mickey's Birthday-land" to celebrate Mickey Mouse's 60th birthday. Although Disney created a stop on the *WDW Railroad* for it (and renamed the train *Mickey's Birthdayland Express* for the duration of the celebration) the land was slated for removal at the end of the 60th birthday celebration. It proved so popular with Guests young and old, however, that Disney decided to keep it. A new show was added and the land was renamed "Mickey's Star-

land" on May 26, 1990. In 1996, the land was updated once again (with the addition of new, more permanent buildings) and renamed "Mickey's Toontown Fair."

108. b.) 4
The four rooms in *Mickey's Country House*, which opened on June 18, 1988, are the bedroom, kitchen, den, and game room. Look for some incredible Hidden Mickeys here! (And find more at www.HiddenMickeysGuide.com)

109. b.) Goofy's Wiseacre Farm
The Barnstormer at Goofy's Wiseacre Farm is a great kiddie roller coaster that's fun for adults, too. You ride through Goofy's cornfield and barn.

110. a.) Mickey
You can find Mickey (and get his autographed photo) in the Judge's Tent out back of his house.

111. b.) Mickey's Hollywood Theatre
Minnie didn't have a home in Toontown Fair until April 15, 1996,

when the land was refurbished and Minnie's home was installed in place of Mickey's Hollywood Theatre (which had opened on June 18, 1988).

112. d.) Aladdin
On the table near the front door of *Mickey's Country House*, you can see letters from pen pals like Buzz Lightyear (his return address is "Infinity and Beyond"), Ariel (send her mail "Under the Sea"), and Wendy from *Peter Pan* (who seems to be writing from "Hook's Room"). There's also a package from Peter Pan labeled, "Use no hooks!" Get it? No "HOOKs"?

113. b.) A propeller
Goofy has two mailboxes – one post is in the ground, while another for "Air Mail" is "propped up" by an airplane propeller. Did you get it? What "props" the mailbox up?

114. c.) Miss Daisy
Donald's Boat opened in Mickey's Toontown Fair on April 15, 1996. The boat, named after Donald's lady friend, is a water play area for chil-

Did You Know?

LOOK AT THE VEGETABLES ON GOOFY'S FARM IN MICKEY'S TOONTOWN FAIR — THE SQUASH ARE FLATTENED OUT AND THE BELL PEPPERS ARE SHAPED LIKE REAL BELLS! GET IT? "SQUASH"? "BELL" PEPPERS?

dren. Be sure to let your kids go inside, turn the Captain's wheel, and blow the ship's whistle. (See what happens outside!)

115. a.) "Trust Me With Your Car"

Painted to the right of the big barn doors on Pete's Garage is the slogan, "Trust Me With Your Car." But don't try to park your car inside; the "garage" is really a restroom!

116. b.) Duckburg University

At *Mickey's Country House*, the radio in the living room is announcing the scores of Mickey's favorite football team, Duckburg University. You can also see a "#1" foam hand and pennants for Duckburg U. in the den (along with a few pennants for "Goofy Tech").

117. b.) *Grandma Duck's Farm*

Goofy's Wiseacre Farm used to be a petting zoo called *Grandma Duck's Farm*. The star attraction was "Minnie Moo," a cow that was born with a big "hidden Mickey" on her flank. When *The Barnstormer* was added to Toontown, the petting zoo, including Minnie Moo, was incorporated into the Tri-Circle D Ranch petting zoo at Fort Wilderness. Minnie Moo passed on to greener pastures in 2002 at the ripe old age of 15.

118. a.) Ludwig von Drake

It was Professor von Drake of the "Old Duck and the Sea Enterprises" who drew the map in *Donald's Boat* of the Quack Sea, Mount Quackmore, the inlets, islands, and the way to Toontown Fair.

The *Hall* contains Cornelius Coot's County Bounty merchandise shop and three character rooms. In the first, Guests can meet classic Disney characters; in the second, Pooh and friends. The third is usually occupied by characters from Disney's latest animated film.

122. b.) Minnie
When "Mickey's Starland" was renamed "Mickey's Toontown Fair" in 1996, *Mickey's House* was spruced up a bit and became *Mickey's Country House*. The neighborhood got even better when Minnie Mouse moved in next door.

119. b.) Ping Pong table
Look for a Hidden Mickey in the Ping Pong paddle in the rec room!

120. d.) Multiflex Octoplane
Blueprints seen in *The Barnstormer* queue reveal that Goofy's design is known as a Multiflex Octoplane, evidencing the facts that this plane is reminiscent of an old crop-duster, is flexible, and has eight passenger sections.

121. b.) Ears of corn
Cornelius Coot, the founder of Toontown Fair, is honored with a statue that sits atop ears of corn in Cornelius Coot Commons in front of the *Toontown Hall of Fame*.

123. a.) Gulp Gas
Take a close look at the gas pump in Pete's Garage. You can see the "keys" to the restroom floating inside!

124. b.) 1 smidgen = 4 oodges
Take a look inside the messy kitchen of Mickey's house: you'll find the plans for his new dishwasher.

125. c.) Duckburg
When what is now called Mickey's Toontown Fair originally opened in 1988, you could visit Mickey in his house, located in the town of Duckburg — a town that was "all that it was quacked up to be," with a population of 'Bill'ions — and still growing." Its founder was Donald Duck's great-great-grandfather, Cornelius Coot. You can still find a

statue honoring him at the entrance to the Judge's Tent.

126. d.) Pull a rope

On *Donald's Boat*, pulling on the rope to sound the ship's whistle also causes a stream of water to shoot out the top of the smokestack.

127. b.) Donald and Goofy

As you look through Mickey's house, you'll see Donald and Goofy along with plenty of evidence of a number of other visitors (look in the den!). It seems that they've all offered to help remodel Mickey's kitchen. (It's the thought that counts, I guess.)

128. c.) A flight school for pets

Walking through the queue of Goofy's *Barnstormer* reveals that it is home to "Fido's Fearless Flight School: Fur Cats and Dogs." Be sure to take a look at the "class schedule" and plane blueprints for a laugh!

Tomorrowland

129. a.) 1995

Tomorrowland was originally designed to portray Disney's view of the future. Unfortunately, a land about the future needs constant (and expensive) updating. Therefore, Disney decided that instead of focusing on the real future, it would look at the "future" as seen by both classic science fiction writers like Jules Verne

and films of the 1920s and 1930s such as *Buck Rogers*. The "New Tomorrowland," heralded as "The Future that Never Was," opened in 1995 with updated attractions, as well as a new look. Gone were the land's original stark white pillars and cold architecture, replaced by colorful, futuristic "retro" icons adorned with metal, neon, and glass.

130. c.) Rover

The poor dog in *Carousel of Progress* must have an identity crisis. He currently answers to "Rover" but has been called "Buster," "Sport," and even "Queenie" over the years. Not only that, his coat has changed from white (at the World's Fair) to light brown to today's dark brown.

131. d.) *Magic Journeys*

The Tomorrowland Circle-Vision Theater has been home to a number of different films since its opening in November 1971, but never to *Magic Journeys*, which is a 3-D film.

132. d.) RCA

RCA was the first official sponsor of *Space Mountain*, backing it from 1975 until 1993, at which time Federal Express took over. It has no corporate sponsor as we go to press.

133. b.) Galactic Hero

During your pre-flight briefing for your mission on *Buzz Lightyear's Space Ranger Spin*, you learn that the Evil Emperor Zurg is stealing Crystollic Fusion Power Units (which look just like "C" batteries to me), and that you and the other Junior Space Rangers must capture him as soon as possible. Then you board your space cruiser and take a quick trip through the Astro Accelerator to outer space. All around you are targets of different sizes, all shaped like the letter "Z." Each target is worth from 100 to 10,000 points (with some bonus, hidden targets scattered along the way). After one final shootout with Emperor Zurg, Buzz Lightyear congratulates you on a Mission Accomplished. Your score is displayed in your ride vehicle. Look for your ranking on the left-hand side just before you exit your vehicle and step onto the speed ramp. Rankings range from Space Cadet (1,000 to 9,999 points) all the way up to Galactic Hero (900,000 to 999,999 points).

134. d.) None
A bit of a trick question, but you did not need a ticket to get into *If You Had Wings*. It was free!

135. d.) 6
Each of the six theaters in *Walt Disney's Carousel of Progress* rotates around a center stage, transporting 240 Guests per theater through time as they follow a growing family embracing new technologies.

136. b.) *Mission to Mars*
The ExtraTERRORestrial Alien Encounter was located in the building that originally housed the D-ticket attraction *Flight to the Moon*. *Flight to the Moon* was updated and reopened on June 7, 1975, as *Mission to Mars*, which in turn, took its last flight to the Red Planet on October 4, 1993. *The ExtraTERRORestrial Alien Encounter* took its place in 1995 when the "New Tomorrowland" opened. If rumor is to be believed, the attraction that opened to the public then was actually a "second version." It's said that when Michael Eisner rode the "first version," he felt it wasn't scary enough. Therefore, the attraction was modified before its official opening. *Alien Encounter* closed in late 2003 and was replaced by *Stitch's Great Escape*.

137. b.) Space Port
Named "Space Port" when it was conceived, the attraction that became *Space Mountain* was originally designed for Disneyland, but it was built in WDW first.

138. a.) Leonard Burnedstar
According to one of the posters you pass as you walk from the Tomorrowland Terrace Noodle Station into Tomorrowland proper, Leonard Burnedstar will be conducting the Martian Pops Orchestra in concert.

139. a.) 2 minutes, 30 seconds
Time flies when you're having fun, right? Although the entire trip lasts less than three minutes and this classic ride has some of the longest lines in the entire park, *Space Mountain* is worth the wait!

140. c.) Tom Morrow
Tom Morrow was the Director of Operations in Mission Control for the *Flight to the Moon* attraction. He was replaced by Mr. Johnson when the ride became *Mission to Mars*. However, Tom Morrow can still be found in Tomorrowland . . . sort of. You can hear his name being paged

while you are riding the *Tomorrowland Transit Authority*: "Paging Mr. Morrow. Mr. Tom Morrow. Your party from Saturn has arrived. Please give them a ring."

141. d.) Yew Nork City
Sonny, the lovable lounge singer at Cosmic Ray's Starlight Café in Tomorrowland, is from Yew Nork City on the planet Zork. Catch some of his hits, such as the "Planetary Boogie," and enjoy such classic jokes as: "Hey! Did you hear the universe is expanding? Guess it's time to loosen the asteroid belt."

142. b.) *Magic Carpet 'Round the World*
The Circle-Vision 360 film, *Magic Carpet 'Round the World,* played at the Tomorrowland Circle-Vision Theatre from March 1974 until March 1975, and again from September 1979 until September 14, 1984. More than 37 hours of film shot in over 20 nations were edited into this panoramic, 21-minute presentation, which took Guests on a virtual journey around the world.

143. b.) 28 mph
While many people believe that *Space Mountain* is the fastest ride in WDW, it isn't even close. It travels at a top speed of about 28 miles per hour, while Epcot's *Test Track* reaches speeds of up to 65 mph. *Space Mountain* isn't even the fastest ride

Did You Know?

THERE'S A PICTURE OF WALT DISNEY ON
THE LEFT WALL OF THE DAUGHTER'S ROOM
IN THE THIRD SCENE OF *CAROUSEL OF PROGRESS*.

in the MK. *Big Thunder Mountain Railroad* averages 30 mph (with a top speed of 33 mph) and *Splash Mountain*'s 87-foot drop takes you up to speeds of 40 mph! The Disneyland Paris *Space Mountain*, however, tops out at about 43.5 mph!

144. c.) Cleveland
The Timekeeper was a Circle-Vision 360 film that opened on November 21, 1994. During his opening address to Guests, Timekeeper welcomed his assistant by saying, "I'd like you all to meet my assistant. She's bold; she's brassy; she's self-contained. All the way from Cleveland, Ohio. Please welcome Miss Self-Programming

Circumvisual Photodroid. Let's say hello to Nine-Eye."

145. c.) Eastern Airlines
Eastern Airlines earned the right to be the official airline of WDW and

an attraction sponsor for a payment rumored to be in the neighborhood of $10 million. By the time WDW opened in 1971, Eastern was providing service to Orlando from 60 major cities across the United States, so Disney had to come up with an attraction to showcase the airline's service to exotic destinations. Disney built *If You Had Wings* in just

Did You Know?

THE ENTIRE PRODUCTION OF
MICKEY'S PHILHARMAGIC WAS CREATED ON COMPUTERS,
REPRESENTING THE FIRST TIME THE CLASSIC
DISNEY CHARACTERS IT FEATURES WERE
FULLY MODELED AND ANIMATED DIGITALLY.

Did You Know?

IF YOU'RE LOOKING FOR SOMEWHERE TO THROW YOUR
GARBAGE IN TOMORROWLAND, YOU MAY JUST FIND THE
MOVING AND TALKING TRASH CAN! HIS NAME IS PUSH.
WALK OVER AND SAY "HI."

28,000 square feet of space on the east side of the existing Circle-Vision 360 Theater building in Tomorrowland. The 10-minute ride used the OmniMover ride system, modeled after the *Adventure Thru Inner Space* attraction in Disneyland (and similar to the one used in *The Haunted Mansion*). *If You Had Wings* opened to the public as a free attraction (no A, B, C, D or E ticket required) on June 5, 1972, and was dedicated less than a month later on July 2. Not only could you ride for free, you could get a free Eastern "wings" pin to commemorate your journey. The ride went through a number of name changes after Eastern withdrew its sponsorship. It was eventually replaced by *Buzz Lightyear's Space Ranger Spin*, which still uses an OmniMover track system.

146. d.) Mel Blanc
Perennial houseguest Cousin Orville can be seen in the bathtub in *Carousel of Progress* reading the paper and wiggling his toes over the edge. Famed Warner Brothers voice artist,

Mel Blanc (ever hear of some guy named "Bugs Bunny"? Hmph. Me neither) provides Orville's voice. Mel stopped by the studios one day in 1963 and voiced Orville — the only voiceover he ever did for Disney, other than contributing some "grunts" for cavemen in the 1964-65 World's Fair Ford Pavilion. When he learned Orville would be smoking a cigar while he soaked, Mel put a pencil in his mouth to add an extra bit of realism to his small part.

147. a.) Sector 9
In the queue for *Buzz Lightyear's Space Ranger Spin*, you can see a map of the planets of the Galactic Alliance, along with your flight path, which will take you from the Star Command Planet at the center of the Gamma Quadrant to Planet Z in Sector 9.

Did You Know?

THE PYRAMID THAT MAKES UP THE MEXICO PAVILION
WAS INSPIRED BY THE 1ST TO 3RD CENTURY
MESOAMERICAN PYRAMIDS IN TEOTIHUACAN, MEXICO,
INCLUDING THE TEMPLE OF QUETZALCOATL
(THE FEATHERED SERPENT).

CHAPTER THREE

EPCOT

1. What does "EPCOT" stand for?
a.) "Peace" in Latin
b.) Exceptional Peace & Cooperation of Today
c.) Experimental Prototype Community of Tomorrow
d.) It is a universal word that translates into "future."

2. Where can you see a model of Walt Disney's original vision for Epcot?
a.) City Hall on Main Street, U.S.A. in the Magic Kingdom
b.) On the *Tomorrowland Transit Authority*
c.) In Innoventions West Side
d.) In *Space Mountain*

3. What was the Epcot theme park originally called?
a.) It has always been called Epcot.
b.) EPCOT Center
c.) Future World
d.) Discoveryland

4. Who dedicated Epcot in 1982?
a.) Roy O. Disney
b.) Michael Eisner
c.) Bob Hope
d.) E. Cardon Walker

5. How much did it cost to construct Epcot?
a.) $1.4 billion
b.) $7 billion
c.) $750,000,000
d.) $955,500,000

6. Which of these countries did NOT attend Disney's official announcement of its "master plan" for EPCOT and World Showcase?
a.) Greece
b.) Israel
c.) Iran
d.) Spain

7. When did groundbreaking begin on Epcot?
a.) January 1, 1980
b.) May 1, 1979
c.) October 1, 1979
d.) October 15, 1971

Future World

8. What was *Horizons* originally going to be called?
a.) *Century 3*
b.) *Mission: SPACE*
c.) *Mission to Mars*
d.) *New Horizons*

9. In *Ellen's Energy Adventure*, what is the IQ of Ellen's old roommate, Judy?
a.) 171
b.) 210
c.) 350
d.) "Off the charts, Alex."

10. How many different Audio-Animatronics figures of Ellen Degeneres can you find in the *Universe of Energy* attraction?

a.) None
b.) 1
c.) 2
d.) 3

11. What is the designation of your rocket in *Mission: SPACE*?
a.) X2
b.) ISTC-71
c.) XP-37
d.) NCC1701

12. *Spaceship Earth*, the icon of Epcot, is often referred to as "the big golf ball." OK then, if *Spaceship Earth* really were a golf ball, how tall would the golfer have to be to match its scale?
a.) 999 feet tall
b.) 1,500 feet tall
c.) 1.2 miles tall
d.) 3 miles tall

13. Who was the first narrator of the *Spaceship Earth* attraction?
a.) Walker Edmiston
b.) Walter Cronkite
c.) Walter Pigeon
d.) Vic Perrin

Did You Know?

0

1

ONE INCH OF WATER SIPHONED OFF THE TOP OF *THE LIVING SEAS* TANK WOULD FILL A REGULAR-SIZED SWIMMING POOL. THAT'S ABOUT 20,000 GALLONS! *THE LIVING SEAS* TANK HOLDS NEARLY 5,700,000 GALLONS!

14. When did *Magic Journeys* close in Epcot?
- a.) 1984
- b.) 1986
- c.) 1990
- d.) 1993

15. What powers your rocket ship to Mars in *Mission: SPACE*?
- a.) Natural gas
- b.) Nuclear fusion
- c.) Solid hydrogen
- d.) Premium unleaded

16. In the "Final Jeopardy" scene of *Ellen's Energy Adventure*, the answer is: "This is one source of energy that will never run out." Ellen's answer is, "What is ___?
- a.) "Solar power"
- b.) "Brain power"
- c.) "The power of imagination"
- d.) "The power of invention"

17. What was used as an inspiration for the ride system in *Soarin'*?
- a.) A child's Erector set
- b.) A flight training simulator
- c.) An Imagineer's love of hang gliding
- d.) A ride an Imagineer saw as a child in Coney Island, New York

18. Which of the following was NOT one of the names of the show in the Universe of Energy pavilion?
- a.) *The Universe of Energy*
- b.) *Ellen's Energy Crisis*
- c.) *Ellen's Energy Adventure*
- d.) *The Exxon Energy Adventure*

19. What did it cost to build *Test Track*?
- a.) Just under $25,000,000
- b.) $75,000,000
- c.) $50,000,000
- d.) Over $100,000,000

20. On *Mission: SPACE*, what is said just before you go into hypersleep?

Did You Know?

SPACESHIP EARTH IS ACTUALLY TWO SPHERES. THE OUTER SPHERE IS ABOUT TWO FEET AWAY FROM THE INNER SPHERE, WHICH HOUSES THE ATTRACTION.

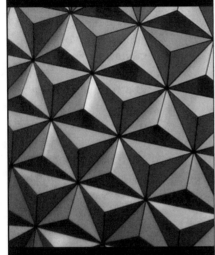

Did You Know?

SPACESHIP EARTH IS 165 FEET IN DIAMETER AND COULD FIT COMPLETELY INSIDE THE TANK IN THE LIVING SEAS, WHICH IS 203 FEET IN DIAMETER—IF YOU REMOVED THE FISH, WATER, AND OTHER CONTENTS.

a.) "Engineer . . . Activate hypersleep . . . NOW!"
b.) "Pleasant dreams."
c.) "See you in a couple of minutes."
d.) "Goodnight."

21. How many people at a time could ride in a *Living Seas* Sea Cab before the ride-through part of the attraction closed?
   a.) 2
   b.) 4
   c.) 6
   d.) 8

22. What was the original name of The Garden Grill restaurant in The Land Pavilion?
   a.) The Circle of Food
   b.) The Good Turn
   c.) The Land Grille Room
   d.) Lunching with The Land

23. As you pass through *Spaceship Earth*, you can view a scene from the film *Snow White and the Seven Dwarfs*. What song is playing during that clip?
   a.) "Whistle While You Work"
   b.) "The Silly Song"
   c.) "Heigh-Ho"
   d.) "I'm Wishing"

24. What is the "Environmental Test #7" in *Test Track*?
   a.) Heat
   b.) Cold

c.) Corrosion
d.) Crash

25. Who plays the Mission Commander who guides you through the *Mission: SPACE* attraction?
a.) Gary Sinese
b.) Gary Oldman
c.) Gary Coleman
d.) Gary U.S. Bonds

26. In *Horizons*, what smell filled the air in the desert scene?
a.) Oranges
b.) Sea water
c.) Lemons
d.) Watermelon

27. What is the fountain in the center of Future World called?
a.) Fountain of Information
b.) A New Hope
c.) Fountain of Nations
d.) Undiscovered Earth

28. The monument that honors famous inventors from history is called ___?
a.) Innovators
b.) Centorium
c.) Legacies
d.) Discoveries

29. How many individual triangles make up the exterior shell of *Spaceship Earth*?
a.) 954
b.) 7,342

c.) 11,324
d.) 19,710

30. The "pilot" who guides you through a 12-year-old's morning in the *Cranium Command* attraction is named what?
a.) Willie
b.) Mickey
c.) Buzzy
d.) Robin

31. What is the name of the assistant who introduces Nigel Channing in the Imagination Institute?
a.) Figment
b.) Cristy Smithers
c.) Eric Idle
d.) Dean Finder

32. Who did actor Jeremy Irons replace as narrator of *Spaceship Earth*?
a.) Walter Cronkite
b.) Walter Pigeon
c.) Vic Perrin
d.) Orson Welles

33. What was the first Future World attraction to be added after the park's opening date?
a.) *Test Track*
b.) *Horizons*
c.) *The Living Seas*
d.) *Journey Into Imagination*

34. Which of the following about *Spaceship Earth* is true?

a.) It is a hemispherical dome.

b.) It is an imperfect sphere.

c.) It was designed by renowned architect James D. Whitson.

d.) It is wider than it is tall.

35. "Mezzo Mix," one of Club Cool's free sample beverages, is from what country?

a.) Italy

b.) Spain

c.) Germany

d.) Portugal

36. The courtyard in front of *Mission: SPACE* is called ___?

a.) SpacePort

b.) Planetary Plaza

c.) Avenue of the Planets

d.) Centorium

37. When did *Horizons* permanently close?

a.) January 9, 1999

b.) October 1, 1989

c.) January 9, 1994

d.) December 31, 1987

38. The film shown in The Land's Harvest Theater stars characters from what Disney movie?

a.) *Lilo and Stitch*

b.) *The Lion King*

c.) *Mulan*

d.) *Finding Nemo*

39. What was the first Future World attraction to have a Kidcot Fun Stop?

a.) *Universe of Energy*

b.) *Living with the Land*

c.) *Test Track*

d.) *Journey Into Imagination*

40. Who discovers fire in Ellen's dream during *Ellen's Energy Adventure*?

a.) Michael Richards (Kramer from TV's *Seinfeld*)

b.) Keith Richards (from the Rolling Stones)

c.) Denise Richards (actress/model)

d.) Little Richard (musician)

41. How many images can eventually be placed on the "Leave a Legacy" statues?

a.) 1,971,000

b.) 198,200

c.) 200,000

d.) 750,000

42. What is the name of the fictional training facility in which the *Mission: SPACE* attraction takes place?

a.) EPCOT Station

b.) Mission to Mars Training Academy

c.) International Space Training Center (ISTC)

d.) WED Interstellar Training Center

43. In *Ellen's Energy Adventure*, who is the announcer in the *Jeopardy!* game show dream sequence?

Did You Know?

THERE ARE OVER 250,000 SPARKLING RED METALLIC "EYE CATCHERS" IN THE WORD "EPCOT" THAT'S NEXT TO THE SORCERER MICKEY ARM AND WAND ON TOP OF *SPACESHIP EARTH*.

a.) Johnny Gilbert
b.) Don Pardo
c.) Ben Stein
d.) Johnny Olsen

44. What was the Imagination! Pavilion originally planned to be about?
a.) Farming
b.) Wind and flight
c.) Ecology
d.) Recycling

45. Which of these famous persons from history is not quoted on the walls of the plaza outside *Mission: SPACE*?
a.) Galileo
b.) Sir Isaac Newton
c.) John F. Kennedy
d.) Socrates

46. Who sponsored *Horizons* from 1983 to 1993?
a.) General Electric
b.) Monsanto
c.) Kodak
d.) Sperry

47. Past recipients of the "Inventor of the Year" award are featured in the pre-show of *Honey, I Shrunk the Audience*. Who of the following is NOT among them?
a.) Thomas Edison
b.) Walt Disney
c.) Alexander Graham Bell
d.) Alexander Eastman

48. What pavilion in Future World was the first to change its corporate sponsor?
a.) *Test Track*
b.) *Horizons*
c.) *The Living Seas*
d.) The Land

49. In *Spaceship Earth*, the actor in the Greek theater scene is delivering lines from a work by what author?
a.) Sophocles
b.) Plato
c.) Aristotle
d.) Mickius Maximus

50. What fictional web site does the announcer tell visitors to go

to if they want to "play the home game" in *Ellen's Energy Adventure*?

a.) energyadventure.org
b.) stupidjudy.com
c.) energynightmare.game
d.) universeofenergy.com

51. Who portrayed the Supreme Leader in *Captain EO*?

a.) Glenn Close
b.) Anjelica Huston
c.) Meryl Streep
d.) Goldie Hawn

52. Guests heard two theme songs during the original *Universe of Energy* attraction. One was titled simply, "Universe of Energy." What was the other called?

a.) "One Little Spark"
b.) "Tomorrow's Child"
c.) "Energy (You Make The World Go 'Round)"
d.) "If We Can Dream It, We Can Do It"

53. What was the name of the dog in *Horizons*?

a.) Napoleon
b.) Caesar
c.) Twiki
d.) Pluto

54. Who led the team that designed the "Leave a Legacy" photo gallery monuments found at the entrance to Future World?

a.) Charlie Ridgway
b.) John Hench
c.) Joe Rohde
d.) Marc Davis

55. What science fiction writer collaborated on *Spaceship Earth*?

a.) Isaac Asimov
b.) Carl Sagan
c.) Gene Roddenberry
d.) Ray Bradbury

56. Disney is known for using smells as well as visuals and sounds to enhance an attraction's experience. How many different scents can you sniff as you ride *Soarin'*?

a.) 0
b.) 2
c.) 3
d.) 5

57. The Wonders of Life Pavilion was originally sponsored by what company?

a.) Exxon
b.) MetLife
c.) Kodak
d.) GE

58. What consolation prize is given to Albert Einstein after he loses in *Jeopardy!* to Ellen Degeneres in *Ellen's Energy Adventure*?

a.) A set of steak knives
b.) A toaster
c.) A light bulb
d.) The *Jeopardy!* home game

59. On the replica of the moon outside the *Mission: SPACE* building, there are red, white, and blue markers. What does the red marker represent?
    a.) The first manned mission into space
    b.) The first unmanned landing on the moon
    c.) It commemorates lives lost in space.
    d.) The first lunar landing

60. What was the name of the robot in a post-ride show of the *World of Motion* attraction?
    a.) Tom Morrow
    b.) Tiger
    c.) Rover
    d.) Rex

61. In what year did *Kitchen Kabaret* in The Land Pavilion close?
    a.) 1984
    b.) 1989
    c.) 1994
    d.) 1999

62. The *Horizons* attraction featured what theme song?
    a.) "Tomorrow's Child"
    b.) "New Horizons"
    c.) "Now Is the Time"
    d.) "If We Can Dream It, We Can Do It"

63. When did *Test Track* open?

Did You Know?

THE ELABORATE, 134-FOOT LONG MURAL AT THE ENTRANCE TO THE LAND PAVILION IS MADE UP OF OVER 150,000 INDIVIDUAL TILES. IT REPRESENTS THE LAYERS OF THE EARTH'S RICH SOIL WITH COLORFUL PIECES MADE FROM GLASS, SLATE, GRANITE, GOLD, AND MARBLE. THE TWO SIDES OF THE MURAL ARE EXACTLY ALIKE, EXCEPT FOR ONE EMERALD GREEN TILE ON THE RIGHT HAND MURAL, PLACED THERE BY THE ARTIST (REPRESENTING HER BIRTHSTONE) AS HER "SIGNATURE."

a.) 1989
b.) 1997
c.) 1999
d.) 2001

64. Who was the first recipient of the "Person of the Century" award, based on votes cast by Guests in CommuniCore?
a.) No One
b.) Walt Disney
c.) John F. Kennedy
d.) Martin Luther King, Jr.

65. What was the theme song to the original boat ride in The Land Pavilion?
a.) "Love the Land"
b.) "Living with the Land"
c.) "This Land Is Your Land"
d.) "Listen to the Land"

World Showcase

66. Which of the following shows once played at Epcot?
a.) *The Best of The Muppets on Parade*
b.) *The Best of Barbie*
c.) *The Best of Michael Flatley's Lord of the Dance*
d.) *The Best of Disney on Broadway*

67. What was the name of Epcot's daytime water show that featured the world's largest daytime fireworks display?
a.) *Surprise in the Skies*
b.) *Fantasy in the Sky*
c.) *Skyleidoscope*
d.) *Wishes*

68. In the original concept phase for World Showcase, where was the United States pavilion going to be located?
a.) On an island in the middle of the World Showcase Lagoon
b.) At the main entrance to World Showcase
c.) Where Spaceship Earth stands today
d.) Next to the International Gateway

69. How many flags grace the "Hall of Flags" in the U.S.A. pavilion?
a.) 13
b.) 44
c.) 50
d.) 76

70. The Viking Playground boat in the Norway pavilion is a prop from what film?
a.) *Waterworld*
b.) *Erik the Viking*
c.) *The 13th Warrior*
d.) *Reign of Fire*

71. What was the name of the outdoor light and music show

Did You Know?

ALMOST 100 DIFFERENT SHADES
OF RED WERE SAMPLED BEFORE
DISNEY'S IMAGINEERS CHOSE
THE COLOR OF THE RED PLANET
IN FRONT OF *MISSION: SPACE*.

that immediately preceded
IllumiNations?
  a.) *Laserphonic Fantasy*
  b.) *A New World Fantasy*
  c.) *Fantasy in the Sky*
  d.) *Carnival de Lumiere*

72. **Disney Legend Buddy Baker composed the theme song for which of the following ___?**
  a.) *Impressions de France*
  b.) *IllumiNations*
  c.) *O! Canada*
  d.) *The Hall of Presidents*

73. **Which of these countries was NOT included in the plan for World Showcase?**
  a.) Equatorial Africa
  b.) Spain
  c.) Israel
  d.) Brazil

74. **What two former U.S. Presidents are depicted by Audio-Animatronics figures during their presidential terms in *The American Adventure* show?**

  a.) George Washington and
    Abraham Lincoln
  b.) Theodore Roosevelt and
    Franklin D. Roosevelt
  c.) Bill Clinton and George W.
    Bush
  d.) Abraham Lincoln and John
    F. Kennedy

75. **Other than age and scale, what is the major difference between the Italy pavilion's design and the original Venetian buildings on which the pavilion is modeled?**
  a.) The bell tower and palace are
    on the wrong sides of the
    square.
  b.) The buildings are the wrong
    color.
  c.) The statues are of Greek, not
    Roman, gods.
  d.) The lion atop one of the
    columns has no wings.

76. **In what year was Epcot's International Gateway created?**

Did You Know?

THE GARDEN GRILL, A REVOLVING RESTAURANT IN THE LAND PAVILION, ROTATES FASTER AT BREAKFAST THAN AT DINNER BECAUSE DISNEY WANTS DINERS TO EXPERIENCE AN ENTIRE REVOLUTION DURING THEIR MEAL AND PEOPLE SPEND LESS TIME EATING BREAKFAST.

a.) 1982
b.) 1983
c.) 1990
d.) 1999

77. What body of water can be reached by boat from World Showcase?
a.) Bay Lake
b.) Crescent Lake
c.) The Seven Seas Lagoon
d.) Hourglass Lake

78. Who initially sponsored *IllumiNations*?
a.) Kodak
b.) Philips Lighting
c.) AT&T
d.) GE

79. What is the Mitsukoshi Department Store in the Japan pavilion named after?
a.) The oldest department store in the world
b.) The first emperor of Japan
c.) The first capital city of Japan

d.) A Japanese saying which means, "honor, pride, culture"

80. Benjamin Franklin, your host for *The American Adventure*, represents the 18th century. Who represents the 20th?
a.) John Glenn
b.) Ronald Reagan
c.) Will Rogers
d.) No One

81. How many nations were represented in World Showcase when Epcot opened in 1982?
a.) 4
b.) 7
c.) 9
d.) 10

82. Which of these time periods is not represented in the UK pavilion's buildings?
a.) 1300s
b.) 1500s
c.) 1600s
d.) 1800s

83. In what year did the Norway pavilion join Epcot's World Showcase?
- a.) 1983
- b.) 1988
- c.) 1993
- d.) 1995

84. What show can be found in the UK pavilion?
- a.) *King Arthur and the Holy Grail*
- b.) *Romeo and Juliet*
- c.) *The Book of Pooh*
- d.) *Alice in Wonderland*

85. If you enter World Showcase from Future World and proceed counterclockwise, which pavilion will you reach first?
- a.) England
- b.) France
- c.) Germany
- d.) Canada

86. What is unique about the stores in the Germany pavilion?
- a.) They are surrounded by water and accessible only by bridge.
- b.) They are designed to look like rooms in a house.
- c.) A model train runs through them on a track close to the ceiling.
- d.) They do not use electronic cash registers.

87. Which nation had its tile work installed by its country's native craftsmen?
- a.) Italy
- b.) Japan
- c.) Morocco
- d.) Norway

88. What orchestra provides *The American Adventure's* music?
- a.) Boston Pops
- b.) New York Symphony

Did You Know?

THE COLOR RED, USED EXTENSIVELY IN THE CHINA PAVILION, SYMBOLIZES HAPPINESS TO THE CHINESE, WHILE GOLD REPRESENTS ROYALTY. THE DRAGON AND PHOENIX SYMBOLS REPRESENT THE EMPEROR AND EMPRESS.

c.) London Philharmonic

d.) Philadelphia Orchestra

89. In what pavilion could you hear holiday stories from a monkey?

a.) Germany

b.) Japan

c.) Norway

d.) China

THE ANSWERS
TO CHAPTER THREE

1. c.) Experimental Prototype Community of Tomorrow

EPCOT has always stood for "Experimental Prototype Community of Tomorrow," the name Walt Disney gave to his original plan for a future-oriented community. However, to many Cast Members past and present, EPCOT has countless other meanings. Among them, "Every Paycheck Comes On Thursday" and "Even Programmers Can't Operate *Test Track*."

2. b.) On the *Tomorrowland Transit Authority*

In 1967, a model of Walt Disney's dream project, the city known as EPCOT, was built and installed as part of a fifth scene for Disneyland's *Carousel of Progress*. It was meant to provide a preview of the city Walt proposed to build on his newly acquired land in Florida. When Disneyland's *Carousel of Progress* closed, the model was sent to WDW and installed in the *Mission to Mars* building in the Magic Kingdom's Tomorrowland. It can only be seen from the *Tomorrowland Transit Authority*. As your train enters the *Stitch*'s building, look for the model on the left hand side.

3. b.) EPCOT Center

The name of the theme park that evolved from Walt Disney's vision of a working city was originally "EPCOT Center." By the time the theme park had been in operation for more than a decade, however, the word "Epcot" was no longer regarded as an acronym, but as an actual word. Therefore, when many of the park's attractions were refurbished in 1994, the word

Did You Know?

THE UK PAVILION
INCLUDES REPLICAS OF
CASTLES THAT BELONGED
TO KING HENRY VIII
AND SIR WALTER SCOTT.

"Center" was removed from the name and the park was renamed "Epcot '94." Well, Disney liked the idea (and the fact that we all now had to buy a new shirt every year), so in 1995, it became, you guessed it . . . "Epcot '95." Thankfully, in 1996 this confusing annual re-naming came to an end, and the park's name became simply "Epcot" (capital E, lower case p, c, o, and t).

4. d.) E. Cardon Walker
EPCOT Center, as the park was initially called, was officially dedicated on October 24, 1982 (23 days after its official opening day) by the late E. Cardon "Card" Walker, a former mailroom worker who went on to become Chairman and CEO of the Disney Corporation.

5. a.) $1.4 billion
After three years of construction, and an outlay of a little over $1.4 billion dollars, EPCOT Center opened to the public on October 1, 1982. A television special hosted

by Danny Kaye took viewers on a tour of the park, with the help of other celebrities and performers. Although nothing like Walt's original visions or designs for EPCOT, Epcot the theme park still reflects his hopes and visions for the future.

6. d.) Spain
When the original "Master Plan" for EPCOT was presented in July 1975, it focused primarily on World Showcase, which it conceived as a permanent, international showplace of cultures, peoples, and products. Dignitaries from nations around the globe attended the presentation. Oddly enough, however, Spain, which at one time was scheduled to have had a pavilion in World Showcase, sent no representative.

7. c.) October 1, 1979
On October 1, 1978, "Card" Walker, then President of Walt Disney Productions, presented the public with drawings and models

of the company's plans for EPCOT, a theme park consisting of Future World and World Showcase, two separate areas of discovery inspired by the dreams of Walt Disney. Exactly one year to the day later, October 1, 1979, groundbreaking began on a 550-acre site about two miles south of the Magic Kingdom (a site Walt Disney himself had identified as the location for the "downtown" area of his planned Community of Tomorrow). The theme park opened just three years later — on, you guessed it, October 1, 1982.

Future World

8. a.) *Century 3*

Horizons, like many WDW attractions, went through several concept revisions and renamings before it was built and premiered. Along the way, its name changed from *Century 3* (or *Century III*) to *Future-Probe* before it became *Horizons*. "Century 3" signified the United States entering its third century as its own nation. It was rejected when Imagineers and executives of GE, the sponsor, realized that the attraction wasn't just for Americans. Then "FutureProbe" was dismissed as having too medical a connotation. Finally, the concept team embraced "Horizons" because they liked the idea that there is always something new on the horizon, and after you reach it, there's another horizon to challenge you.

9. b.) 210

During the *Jeopardy!* sequence of *Ellen's Energy Adventure*, host Alex Trebeck compliments Judy for "blowing away" her opponents. She smugly replies that her IQ is 210.

10. b.) 1

Like it or not, there is just one Audio-Animatronics figure of Ellen found during the Universe of Energy ride. The rest of the time you can only see her on-screen.

11. a.) X2

During your mission, you are enclosed in X2 Deep Space Flight Vehicles. The design of the X2 is based on actual advanced propulsion technology, which could conceivably be used someday to shuttle real astronauts into deep space.

12. c.) 1.2 miles tall

If *Spaceship Earth* were a golf ball, the golfer would have to stand about 1.2 miles high and the hole he would be shooting for would have to be about 417 feet in diameter to be in proportion to the ball. Instead of hitting the ball, say, 200 yards to sink it, our giant golfer would be sending it nearly 134 miles — approximately the width of Florida. FORE!!!

13. d.) Vic Perrin

Vic Perrin, Walker Edmiston, and Walter Pigeon have all been identified as the original narrator of *Spaceship Earth*. However, the honor actually went to the late Vic Perrin. Perrin may be best known as the "Control Voice" from TV's *The Outer Limits*, which ran from 1963 to 1965. He narrated *Spaceship Earth* until 1986, when the ride underwent a minor refurbishment that included the addition of numerous scenes and a new theme song. It reopened May 26, 1986, with Walter Cronkite as narrator. Jeremy Irons succeeded the famous newsman in November 1994, when the ride was tweaked a second time. Walker Edmiston can be heard in Epcot as the voice of Andrew Carnegie in *The American Adventure* show.

14. b.) 1986

The film *Magic Journeys* examined the world through the eyes of children. It opened with the park on October 1, 1982, and closed on February 9, 1986. It was replaced in the Imagination! Pavilion by Michael Jackson's *Captain EO* in September of that same year. *Magic Journeys* was directed by Murray Lerner, who won an Oscar for his 1980 documentary film, *From Mao to Mozart: Isaac Stern in China*.

15. c.) Solid hydrogen

Did You Know?

IF YOUR *TEST TRACK* RIDE SEEMS A LITTLE "EXTRA BUMPY," IT'S INTENTIONAL. THE TIRES, SPECIALLY DESIGNED AND PROVIDED BY GOODYEAR, ARE FILLED TO 70 POUNDS PER SQUARE INCH INSTEAD OF THE USUAL 35 PSI.

During the preflight movie, you are told by your CapCom that the shuttle is powered by solid hydrogen. This evidences the National Aeronautics and Space Administration's (NASA) cooperation with Disney on the development of *Mission: SPACE*. Solid hydrogen fuel, as well as aerospace rocket engines and hypersleep, are technologies mentioned in the attraction that NASA is actively pursuing.

16. b.) "Brain power"

As Ellen prepares for the "Final Jeopardy" round, the ride cars move back into the original theater. Faced with the question, "What source of power will never run out?" Ellen answers, "What is brain power?" and wins the game. Oh, and what was her roommate Judy's answer? Nothing; she left it blank.

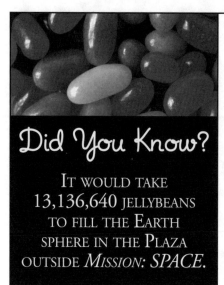

Did You Know?

IT WOULD TAKE 13,136,640 JELLYBEANS TO FILL THE EARTH SPHERE IN THE PLAZA OUTSIDE *MISSION: SPACE*.

17. a.) A child's Erector set
Disney Imagineer Mark Sumner, from the Ride Mechanical Engineering division, had the initial concept for what would become the *Soarin'* attraction. Over a Thanksgiving weekend, he took out an old Erector set and with the help of glue, rubber bands, and other household materials, had a mock-up built of his proposed *Soarin'* ride system in about 3.5 hours. While the model used hand cranking to move the seats, the actual attraction uses a 1,000 hp electrical motor to move the ride system's 1,000,000 pounds of steel.

18. d.) *The Exxon Energy Adventure*
The Universe of Energy was one of Epcot's original pavilions and housed a show of the same name. On September 15, 1996, the show was revised and reopened as *Ellen's Energy Crisis*, a name that was quickly changed to the current title, *Ellen's Energy Adventure*.

19. d.) Over $100,000,000
That's right. *Test Track* cost over 100 million dollars to build. Oh, and do you really think it was built solely for the entertainment of WDW Guests? Think again. The project was a well-conceived marketing tool for its sponsor, General Motors. Where else could GM give 25,000 or more enthusiastic Guests (and potential GM car buyers) a 45-minute introduction to its products every day of the year!

20. a.) "Engineer . . . Activate hypersleep . . . NOW!"
During your journey to the Red Planet, you are put into hypersleep for your long trip. Right before it's time to sleep, your CapCom points out the nearby space station as you prepare for your slingshot around the moon. He then states, "Beautiful sight, isn't it? Something to dream about on the way to Mars . . . Engineer . . . Activate hypersleep . . . NOW!"

21. a.) 2
For many years, Guests who entered *The Living Seas* were shown a film about the formation of the oceans

before boarding a "Hydrolator" to the ocean bottom. There they traveled along a 400-foot tunnel in "Sea Cabs" — small, blue, two-passenger shuttles that allowed Guests to view the ocean, reefs, and marine life close-up through eight-inch thick glass. The ride ended at the Seabase Concourse, which featured hands-on displays and educational exhibits. Sadly, the Sea Cabs were closed on October 21, 2001, for unspecified reasons and it is unknown if they will ever reopen.

22. b.) The Good Turn

Like many of the eateries in The Land Pavilion, the original table-service restaurant has been renamed a number of times since the pavilion's opening. It opened as The Good Turn on October 1, 1982, and then became the Land Grille Room in 1986. Today it is known as The Garden Grill and offers Character Dining. Whatever its name, the restaurant has (literally) revolved around the boat ride below since its opening.

23. b.) "The Silly Song"

While passing through the scene (with the Cinema on the right side of your vehicle), watch the screen for clips from some famous Disney films, such as *20,000 Leagues Under the Sea* and the classic animated tale, *Snow White and the Seven Dwarfs*. The Dwarfs are singing their "Silly Song" — "Ho-la-la-ee-ay, Ho-la-la-ee-ay, Ho-la-la-ee-ay-ee-la-ee-ay-ee-lee-ay . . ."

24. c.) Corrosion

During *Test Track*'s pre-show movie, you are introduced to Bill, up in GM's Control Center. He orders some tests to be done to the ride vehicle, including #2, #5, and #7. Sherry, the technician, questions whether to subject Guests to test #7, inasmuch as it involves corrosive

Did You Know?

TIGER, THE ROBOT IN THE POST-RIDE SHOW OF *WORLD OF MOTION*, WAS THE FIRST AUDIO-ANIMATRONICS FIGURE TO ACTUALLY PICK UP OBJECTS. HE COULD RETRIEVE CERTAIN ITEMS LOCATED IN HIS BAG.

conditions. The other two environmental tests you encounter are extreme heat and cold.

25. a.) Gary Sinese
Talented actor Gary Sinese had a long-running career before exploding into public notoriety in 1994 with his performance in Stephen King's TV miniseries *The Stand*. He's no stranger to space adventure; he played astronaut Ken Mattingly in the movie, *Apollo 13*.

26. a.) Oranges
A machine called a "Smellitizer" filled the air with the scent of fresh oranges in this bygone attraction. The patented technology wasn't just used at *Horizons*, either. Take a walk down Main Street, U.S.A. in the Magic Kingdom. Smell those incredible chocolate chip cookies? Well, those aren't real cookies you're smelling, so don't try swiping one from the little kid in front of you. The smell comes from a "Smell-

itizer," which in this case pipes the man-made scent of chocolate chip cookies into the outside air through a vent directly over the door to the Main Street Bakery. So you may be able to pass the sign for the bakery, but you just can't resist that smell. Can you think of other attractions that might use the Smellitizer? How about *Ellen's Energy Adventure*? Smell the sulfur in the Mesozoic Era? Yup, that's from a Smellitizer, too!

27. c.) Fountain of Nations
Located behind *Spaceship Earth* and directly across from the Fountainview Café, the Fountain of Nations takes its name from the fact that when Epcot first opened, representatives of nations from around the world brought water from their countries and poured it into the fountain as a symbol of global unity. The fountain displays a computer-controlled water ballet set to music every 15 minutes.

28. d.) Discoveries

This marker, set in the ground near Innoventions, consists of five circles bearing quotations from, and the names and lifespans of, famous inventors, mathematicians, educators, and others who have contributed to the betterment of mankind. Among those names: American philosopher John Dewey; light-bulb inventor Thomas Edison; Sir Isaac Newton, who formulated the laws of gravity, and physicist Marie Curie, who discovered radium in collaboration with her husband, Pierre.

29. c.) 11,324

There are 11,324 triangular facets on the skin of *Spaceship Earth*, made up of 954 interconnected, triangular panels, which are various sizes and angles. This outer skin is made of alucobond, a polyethylene core sandwiched between two anodized aluminum plates. It is self-cleaning and designed to withstand the harsh Florida climate. The globe encloses 2.2 million cubic feet of space and is 165 feet in diameter.

30. c.) Buzzy

The animated short film, *Cranium Command*, follows Buzzy, a rookie recruit in the Cranium Commando forces. Buzzy was called "Captain Cortex" in the 1987 concept design by X. Atencio. Before the attraction opened in 1989, however, his name was changed to "Buzzy."

31. b.) Cristy Smithers

As you enter the pre-show area for the *Honey, I Shrunk the Audience* attraction, you are presented with a number of video screens with the "Inventor of the Year Award" and the Imagination Institute's logo on them. Overhead, you can hear a woman's voice testing the microphone. She then introduces herself as Christy Smithers, an assistant at the Institute. Before the main show begins, she introduces you to her boss, the head of the Imagination Institute, Dr. Nigel Channing, played by Eric Idle.

32. a.) Walter Cronkite

English actor Jeremy Irons replaced Walter Cronkite as *Spaceship Earth* narrator on November 23, 1994, when the attraction reopened after a refurbishment.

33. d.) *Journey Into Imagination*

Although the Imagination! Pavilion opened with the park on October 1, 1982, the only attractions it offered at the time were *Image Works* and the 3-D film, *Magic Journeys*. The *Journey Into Imagination* ride did not open until March 5, 1983. *Horizons* opened later that same year, along with the *New World Fantasy Show* and the Epcot Outreach & Teachers Center. *The Living Seas* opened on January 15, 1986, and *Test Track* on March 17, 1999.

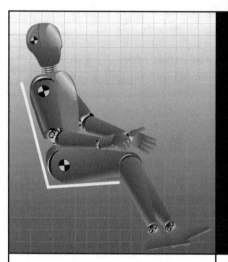

34. b.) It is an imperfect sphere.
Spaceship Earth is 180 feet tall and 165 feet in diameter, making it an imperfect sphere. Counting the 50-ton Mickey hand, wand, and "Epcot" logo (which originally included a 36-foot high "2000" for the Millennium Celebration, for which the hand, wand, and logo were added), the entire structure is over 250 feet high.

35. c.) Germany
Club Cool, located in Innoventions Plaza on the West Side of Epcot, allows you to sample free (yes, I said "free") Coca-Cola drinks from around the globe. In addition to Mezzo Mix, you can sample such flavors as Smart Watermelon, Kinfey Lemon, Diet Tai, Guarana Vegitabeta, Lift Apple, Beverly, and Krest Ginger Ale. Be warned . . . they aren't what you might expect!

36. b.) Planetary Plaza
The welcome center for *Mission: SPACE*, known as Planetary Plaza, took two years to construct. It contains giant spheres representing Earth's moon and planets in our solar system, as well as quotations from persons who have contributed to the success of space travel throughout history.

37. a.) January 9, 1999
Horizons opened on October 1, 1983, exactly one year to the day after Epcot's grand opening. Its sponsor bowed out in 1993, but Disney continued to operate the attraction until late 1994. After being closed for a number of months, *Horizons* reopened in December of 1995 to give the west side of Epcot more attractions while *Universe of Energy* and *World of Motion* were closed for renovation. *Horizons*

closed for good on January 9, 1999, and was completely demolished by October 2000.

38. b.) *The Lion King*
The original movie, *Symbiosis*, was replaced in 1995 by *Circle of Life: An Environmental Fable* starring *The Lion King's* Timon, Pumbaa, and Simba. This 20-minute film demonstrates the dangers facing the environment and the responsibility we all have to care for the land.

39. c.) *Test Track*
Kidcot Fun Stop activity kiosks located in World Showcase and Future World offer school-age kids a fun way to learn more about host nations and pavilion themes and participate in interesting activities. First seen in World Showcase as part of the Millennium Celebration, the Kidcot Fun Stops moved into Future World in 2004, when *Test Track* set up a Fun Stop. As we go to press, the Land and Living Seas pavilions also provide them.

40. a.) Michael Richards (Kramer from TV's *Seinfeld*)
Michael Richards plays man in different evolutionary stages in Ellen's dream during *Ellen's Energy Adventure*. Although most commonly recognized for his role as "Cosmo Kramer," Richards has also appeared in numerous motion pictures. Although he never appeared on the series, he was originally cast in 1986 as "Al Bundy" on the Fox TV series, *Married With Children*. (Rent the 1989 "Weird Al" film, *UHF*; Richards steals the show as dopey janitor, Stanley Spadowski.)

41. d.) 750,000
The 35 "Leave a Legacy" megaliths in Future World's entrance plaza range from 3 to 19 feet high and weigh as much as 50,000 pounds. There is enough room on these structures for 750,000 images.

42. c.) International Space Training Center (ISTC)
Mission: SPACE takes place at the 45,000 square-foot ISTC in the year 2036, 75 years after Yuri Gargarin became the first man in space. The ISTC is a fictional joint venture of many nations that are enthusiastic about exploring space.

43. a.) Johnny Gilbert
A game show announcer and host, Gilbert has one of the most recognizable voices on TV. He hosted *Beat the Odds* and substituted for Bob Barker on the *Price is Right*. But he is most often recognized as the announcer for *The $25,000 Pyramid, Family Feud, Jeopardy!*, and *Wheel of Fortune*. Listen for his recognizable voice as your car moves into the final theater and he instructs you on what to do if you would like to have your own energy nightmare.

44. c.) Ecology
The original plan for the Imagination! Pavilion was an Ecology pavilion. Next door, where The Land Pavilion now sits, was to be a pavilion devoted to forests. You can see a small sampling of what the Forest pavilion might have included in the "Forests For Our Future" exhibit at Innoventions.

45. d.) Socrates
Ten quotations from space explorers and supporters of space exploration line the walls of the plaza outside *Mission: SPACE*. Socrates does not provide one, but his most famous student, Plato, is immortalized in the quotation, "Look upward . . . From this world to the heavens." The famous astronomer and physicist, Galileo Galilei (1564-1642) is quoted as saying, "The Universe . . . stands continually open to our gaze," while U.S. President John F. Kennedy says, "We set sail on this new sea because there is knowledge to be gained. . ."

46. a.) General Electric
General Electric's corporate sponsorship contract for *Horizons* expired on September 30, 1993. The attraction continued to operate until late 1994, however, when it closed temporarily, reopening in 1995 without a sponsor. The ride closed permanently in 1999.

47. c.) Alexander Graham Bell
Among the past honorees are: George Washington Carver, Thomas Edison, Alexander Eastman, and Walt Disney. Professor Wayne Szalinski is being inducted as the newest "Inventor or the Year."

48. d.) The Land
The Land was presented by Kraft General Foods from Epcot's opening day through September 30, 1992. Nestlé USA picked up the sponsorship in November 1992 and has sponsored it ever since. In October 1993, the entire Land Pavilion closed for a few weeks for renovations, re-opening in mid December.

49. a.) Sophocles
The actor in *Spaceship Earth* is performing lines from Sophocles' *Oedipus Rex*. The attention to detail this demonstrates is often overlooked by the casual Guest, but it evidences the Imagineers' commitment to authenticity. Many other such details can be found in this attraction, among them:
• In the scene in ancient Egypt, the hieroglyphics on the walls are recreations of actual writings, while the pharaoh's letter held by one of the figures is a duplicate of an actual letter sent by an Egyptian pharaoh to one of his agents.
• Graffiti found in the ruins of Pompeii are duplicated in the

Spaceship Earth's Roman scene.
• The Islamic scene includes a replica of a 10th century quadrant, a device used in navigation and astronomy.
• The musical instruments in the Renaissance scene are intricately detailed replicas of a Renaissance lute and a lyra de braccio, while the Bible Johann Gutenberg is inspecting is an exact copy of a page of an original Gutenberg bible and the printing press he is "using" has real movable type.
• In the 19th century scene, the steam press is an exact replica of one developed by William Bullock in 1863, and the Morse code message coming into the telegraph office announces the driving of the golden spike at Promontory Peak in 1869 — the event that linked America's transcontinental railroad.

50. c.) energynightmare.game

Listen for the announcement near the end of the attraction. As your ride vehicle moves into the last theater, the *Jeopardy!* theme music begins to play. You'll see Judy and Ellen writing their answers on the screens above you. The *Jeopardy!* announcer then advises that if you'd like to have your own "energy nightmare," all you need do is place a self-addressed, stamped envelope under your pillow, or visit them on the Web at: www.energynightmare.game.

Did You Know?

THE DIFFERENCE IN TEMPERATURE BETWEEEN THE HOT AND COLD TEST ROOMS IN *TEST TRACK* IS 100 DEGREES FAHRENEHIT!

51. b.) Anjelica Huston

In *Captain EO*, Huston plays the film's villain, a wicked queen called the "Supreme Leader." You may know her from her roles in movies such as *The Addams Family* and *Prizzi's Honor* (for which she won a Best Supporting Actress Oscar).

52. c.) "Energy (You Make The World Go 'Round)"

The song was written by Robert Moline and played during the pre-show movie of the same name. The film, showing images of energy production, was projected onto a 14- by 90-foot screen made up of 100 rotating projection triangles that could move and rotate in sync (a process dubbed a "kinetic mosaic" by its creator, Czech filmmaker Emil Radok). The song "Universe of Energy," by Al Kasha and Joel Hirschorn, was the "official theme song" of the original attraction. It was played as the ride cars moved into the final room

of the attraction. The songs were dropped when the attraction was updated in 1996.

53. a.) Napoleon

During *Horizons'* look into the future, a family and their dog have just arrived at Brava Centauri, a space station. As they get off their shuttle and onto the station, the son, Tommy, loses one of his magnetic shoes. As he begins to "float," his mother explains that he, his teddy bear, and his dog (which he is still holding by the leash) are "flying" due to the lack of gravity. Laughing, the mother says not to let go of his dog, Napoleon, as she doesn't want to lose him. His father can be seen "walking" on the top of the station trying to retrieve the lost shoe, as Tommy asks if they can get "mag-shoes" for Napoleon as well.

54. b.) John Hench

The "Leave a Legacy" sculptures were designed by a team of Imagineers led by veteran John Hench, the original art director for Epcot. Hench joined Disney in 1939 as a sketch artist for *Fantasia*. He later expanded his role into layout, background painting, animation effects, and supervision. His work can be seen in such films as *Dumbo, The Three Caballeros, Cinderella, Peter Pan,* and *20,000 Leagues Under The Sea.* At Walt Disney's personal request, Hench joined Walt Disney Imagineering in 1954 as a project designer for Disneyland's Tomorrowland. He developed many of the attractions for that park, as well as shows for the 1964-65 World's Fair. He also provided creative direction for all phases of WDW. He was later named Senior Vice President of Walt Disney Imagineering.

Did You Know?

THE U.S.A. PAVILION COMBINES ARCHITECTURAL ELEMENTS FROM THE ENGLISH GEORGIAN AND NEOCLASSICAL STYLES FOUND IN BUILDINGS SUCH AS PHILADELPHIA'S INDEPENDENCE HALL, BOSTON'S OLD STATE HOUSE, THOMAS JEFFERSON'S HOME, MONTICELLO, AND VARIOUS BUILDINGS IN VIRGINIA'S COLONIAL WILLIAMSBURG.

55. d.) Ray Bradbury
Bradbury, the author of such classic novels as *Fahrenheit 451, The Martian Chronicles,* and *Dandelion Wine,* developed many of the ideas for *Spaceship Earth.* (Other collaborators included the Smithsonian Institute, numerous technical specialists, and consultants from a number of notable universities.) Bradbury also contributed to the conception of the *Orbitron* space ride at Disneyland Paris and wrote the basic concept for the U.S. pavilion at the 1964 New York World's Fair.

56. c.) 3
Your *Soarin'* hang-gliding adventure takes you through California orange groves and pine-scented forests, and delights you with ocean breezes.

57. b.) MetLife
The Wonders of Life Pavilion, located between the *Universe of Energy* and what is now *Mission: SPACE,* opened on Epcot's West Side on October 19, 1989. Physical fitness was the central theme of this domed pavilion, which has featured thrill rides like *Body Wars,* two

celebrity-filled films, and the Fitness Fairgrounds, an area where you could test your senses and evaluate your athletic abilities at various exhibits. When Epcot opened in 1982, plans for a health and physical fitness pavilion had been drawn up, but there was no interested corporate sponsor. Finally, an agreement was made with insurance giant MetLife that allowed the Wonders of Life Pavilion to open — at a cost of over $100,000,000! MetLife ended its sponsorship of the pavilion in June 2001, and all references to it were removed within a month.

58. c.) A light bulb
Einstein is told, "It's a long lasting, low energy light bulb. Enjoy the efficiency!"

59. d.) The first lunar landing
The single red marker marks where Apollo 11 landed on July 20, 1969, and man first stepped on the moon.

60. b.) Tiger
The TransCenter, *World of Motion*'s post-show display area, offered exhibits and two shows, the "Water Engine Show" and the popular "Bird and The Robot" show. Viewed by over seven million Guests a year, "Bird and The Robot" was a comedy and music show hosted by an Audio-Animatronics toucan called "Bird." He and Tiger demonstrated the importance of robots in modern automobile assembly. Tiger performed a variety of tricks for Guests, including "rolling over," "playing dead," and conducting a symphony orchestra, while Bird entertained the audience with silly jokes.

61. c.) 1994
Kitchen Kabaret was a show in The Land Pavilion dedicated to education and entertainment by and about the four major food groups. It closed January 3, 1994, and was replaced by *Food Rocks* less than three months later, on March 26.

62. b.) "New Horizons"
Conceived as a "sequel" to the Magic Kingdom's *Carousel of Progress, Horizons* gave Guests the opportunity to see visions of the future from the past and present. Its theme song, "New Horizons," was written by George Wilkins and sung by Gloria Kaye. The song's refrain quoted the attraction's motto, "If we can dream it, we can do it."

63. c.) 1999
Test Track opened (a little late) nearly two years after the scheduled date of May 1997. What caused the delay? Oh, a few little problems with the ride vehicles. The wheels could not stand up to the rigors of the ride, and the sophisticated computer systems were continually shutting down. Solving those problems required redesigning the wheels and completely redeveloping the computer software — which took Imagineers about a year and a half. Finally, on March 17, 1999, "A New Ride for the New Year" had its Grand Opening. With much fanfare and music by Earth, Wind and Fire and The Spinners, NASCAR driver Richard Petty (with the help of a little "eye candy" that included supermodels Christie Brinkley, Angie Everhart, Carol Alt, and Frederique) officially opened the ride, while fireworks exploded in the sky.

64. a.) No One
Beginning January 14, 1990 (and scheduled to have lasted until January 1, 2000), Future World Guests could vote for the most influential "Person of the Century" at various kiosks in the CommuniCore buildings. Voters could choose from a list of 89 nominees or write in a choice. After four months, the leading nominees were (in alphabetical order) the Beatles, Winston Churchill, Walt Disney, Thomas Edison, Albert Einstein, Henry Ford, Mikhail Gorbachev, John F. Kennedy, Martin Luther King, Jr., and Franklin D. Roosevelt. However, we'll never know who might have won because after a little more than a year, the voting machines were simply removed. Rumors blamed Guest write-ins, but the real reason was Cast Member write-ins. The story is: The employees . . . I mean, Cast Members . . . at Epcot thought it would be funny if they all wrote in the same person's name — allegedly of another Cast Member. Well, I guess these guys had a lot of free time, because before you

know it, the write-ins got out of hand and their phantom nominee was moving high up the rankings — and FAST! It wasn't long before Disney execs found out, and needless to say, they weren't pleased. Things only got worse when they discovered that although they could remove the mystery name, they would also wipe out the entire 18 months' worth of votes! So, hoping no one would notice or ever ask, Disney literally pulled the plug on the whole thing in March of 1991!

65. d.) "Listen to the Land"
"Listen to the Land" was the theme song for a boat ride of the same name. The ride opened with Epcot in 1982 and continued operating until September 27, 1993. Then it reopened in December as *Living with the Land*, with some changed scenes (most notably the beginning and ending) and a new soundtrack,

and without the old theme song.

World Showcase

66. c.) *The Best of Michael Flatley's Lord of the Dance*
Michael Flatley brought his high-energy Irish step-dancing show to Epcot for 16 weeks during the summer of 1999. The show, featuring 50 performers, included numbers from the original production that debuted in Dublin, Ireland, in 1996. It played at the America Gardens Theatre from June until October of 1999, and returned in June of the following year due to its enormous success. It ended its WDW run on August 26, 2000.

67. a.) *Surprise in the Skies*
This special water and air show

debuted in World Showcase on October 1, 1991, to celebrate WDW's 20th anniversary. The show featured boats, hang gliders, jet skis, and paraplanes piloted by Mickey, Minnie, Pluto, Goofy, Chip, Dale, Pooh, and Tigger, along with a gigantic line of kites and giant "jack-in-the-boxes" filled with character balloons. The last were located in front of the nations' pavilions, and they opened to reveal giant balloons shaped like Mickey, Minnie, and 10 other characters. Each balloon was themed to the nation it represented. Goofy's balloon, located in front of the Norway pavilion, for example, resembled a Viking. The show closed with a spectacular fireworks display, which was, at the time, the world's largest. Music from the "Air Battle" sequence of the performance, composed by John Debney, can still be heard intermittently at the Innoventions fountain in Future World.

68. b.) At the main entrance to World Showcase

When World Showcase was in its development phase, the U.S. pavilion was conceived as a large glass building located at the main entrance, with Canada and Mexico on either side (reflecting their geographic location to the north and south of the U.S). Actually, there were questions early on as to whether to have an American pavil-

ion at all! The next plan, to put it at the entrance/exit to Future World, was abandoned for a number of reasons: The large pavilion would block the view of the lagoon and other nations' pavilions; putting the U.S. "front and center" would likely appear chauvinistic; and a large glass building would not make a good transition between Future World and World Showcase. Since they were changing its location, the Imagineers also decided to change the building's design to the Colonial style we see today.

69. b.) 44

As you proceed into *The American Adventure* show, you pass through the "Hall of Flags." It displays a total of 44 flags that have flown over the country from the Revolutionary War and Colonial period on, including the flags of foreign countries that once claimed parts of what's now the U.S.A.

70. c.) *The 13th Warrior*

The 1999 Disney/Touchstone Pictures film, *The 13th Warrior*, was based on the Michael Crichton book, *Eaters of the Dead*, which was adapted from Viking folklore. The film, directed by John McTiernan, tells the story of an emissary (played by Antonio Banderas) who is abducted by a band of warriors. He is forced to join their quest to battle mysterious creatures who,

Did You Know?

THE PRAYER TOWER NEAR THE
ENTRANCE TO THE MOROCCO
PAVILION IS A REPLICA OF THE
KATOUBIA MINARET IN MARRAKESH.

according to legend, consume every living thing in their path.

71. a.) *Laserphonic Fantasy*
Laserphonic Fantasy, the park's first lagoon show, opened on June 9, 1984. It ran until January 29, 1998, when it was replaced by *IllumiNations*. *Laserphonic Fantasy* featured music by Don Dorsey called the "Festival of Festivals," which was originally used for the opening of EPCOT Center in 1982.

72. a.) *Impressions de France*
Buddy Baker joined Disney in 1954 to assist George Bruns, who was working as a composer at the Walt Disney Studios. When George became overloaded, he asked Buddy to help out with *Davy Crockett*. Well, Buddy came to help out for 2 weeks and ended up staying for 29 years. He and George were the sole composers for Disneyland for the park's first 10 years. He was also the musical director for *The Mickey Mouse Club* and wrote scores and songs for

other TV series and films, as well as Disney's theme parks. Buddy's favorite of the attractions he worked on was *Impressions de France* for the France pavilion, for which he combined classical French masterpieces with his own compositions. His best-known work, however, may be "Grim Grinning Ghosts," the theme to Disneyland and WDW's *The Haunted Mansion*. Buddy was the 1999 recipient of the "ASCAP Foundation Lifetime Achievement Award." He died at age 84 in 2002.

73. d.) Brazil
Many concepts for World Showcase pavilions that never made it past the drawing board. There were at various times "coming soon" signs in World Showcase for Israel, Africa, and Spain. None arrived.

74. b.) Theodore Roosevelt and Franklin D. Roosevelt
Theodore Roosevelt and Franklin D. Roosevelt are the only Presidents represented by Audio-Animatronics figures during their terms

as President. Theodore Roosevelt is seen speaking with naturalist John Muir about the beauty of America and its destruction due to industries such as logging. Franklin D. Roosevelt is depicted giving his famous "The only thing we have to fear is fear itself" speech in 1929. George Washington and Thomas Jefferson are also depicted, but during times in their lives before they became President.

75. a.) The bell tower and palace are on the wrong sides of the square. The placement of the Doge's Palace and the Campanile San Marco in the Italy pavilion are reversed from where they actually stand in St. Mark's Square in Venice. Both, however, are exact 1/4-scale replicas of the original buildings. The original Doge's Palace was constructed between 1309 and 1424. It was, at one time, the seat of government, Palace of Justice, and the home of the Doge (chief magistrate) of

the Republic of Venice. (Doges ruled from 697 A.D. until about 1789 A.D.) The Campanile, by far the tallest building in Venice, was originally built as a lighthouse. It was from the top of the Campanile in 1609 that Galileo demonstrated to the Doge how his telescope worked. The original tower collapsed on July 14, 1902, when its foundation gave way. It was rebuilt on the same spot — making the structures in both Venice and WDW replicas of the original.

76. c.) 1990
The International Gateway, located in World Showcase between the UK and France pavilions, puts the theme park an easy walk away from Disney's BoardWalk and the Epcot resorts. Although World Showcase doesn't usually open until

Did You Know?

THE LEFTMOST TOTEM POLE AS YOU FACE THE
CANADA PAVILION IS THE ONLY ONE OF THE THREE THAT
IS REAL. THE 30-FOOT POLE WAS CREATED BY TSIMSHIAN
INDIAN CARVER, DAVID BOXLEY, AND TELLS A STORY OF
RAVEN TRICKING THE CHIEF OF THE SKIES.

11:00 AM, you can use Epcot's "back door" earlier to gain access to Future World.

77. b.) Crescent Lake
Guests can take water taxis between World Showcase and the docks that serve Disney's BoardWalk and the Epcot resort hotels, all of which border Crescent Lake. Plans to construct resorts near Epcot began early on. Designers felt that they should surround a body of water, much as the Magic Kingdom resorts border the Seven Seas Lagoon. To this end, workers dug out a 25-acre area to create the lake. The first hotels built lakeside were the WDW Swan and WDW Dolphin, which opened eight years after the park in 1990. The Yacht and Beach Club Resorts followed soon thereafter, with the BoardWalk Inn and Villas opening a few years later, on July 1, 1996. Disney's Board-Walk, an incredible re-creation of turn-of-the-century Atlantic City and Coney Island, stretches along

a wooden promenade overlooking the lake. It is packed with shops, restaurants, and entertainment.

78. d.) GE
When GE partnered with Disney for the new nighttime fireworks show to replace *Laserphonic Fantasy* in January 1988, lights were added to each of the World Showcase pavilions except Morocco and Norway. Additionally, the fireworks display was greatly enhanced, fountains were added, and a new soundtrack was created and recorded by the Toronto Symphony Orchestra.

79. a.) The oldest department store in the world
The original Mitsukoshi store dates back three centuries. Today's stores are located throughout Asia and are often huge. The Shin Kong Mitsukoshi Department Store in Taichung, Taiwan, for example, has 20 floors, 22 elevators, and 56 escalators. Epcot's version is just a bit smaller, but you'll still find a large

variety of Japanese goods, including "Hello Kitty" and anime items.

80. d.) No One
When the Disney Imagineers were developing *The American Adventure* attraction for Epcot, the original concept called for three hosts — one from each of the centuries of the United States' existence. Choosing the 18th and 19th century hosts was relatively easy: Ben Franklin not only played a major role in American history, but was felt to have had keen insight and the gift of invention, while Mark Twain's wry humor, coupled with his very rational and logical thought processes, made him Franklin's perfect match for the 19th century. However, after initially choosing Will Rogers to host the 20th century, the Imagineers decided that the century's events and achievements could not be embodied by any one individual, and so they dropped the idea of having a 20th century host.

81. c.) 9
World Showcase opened in 1982 with the pavilions of nine nations surrounding the World Showcase Lagoon. The nations were Canada, China, France, Germany, Italy, Japan, Mexico, the United Kingdom (UK), and the U.S.A.

82. a.) 1300s
The buildings in the UK pavilion in World Showcase each possess unique architectural elements. The Tea Caddy building is representative of 1500s' architectural style. The Cantalier Building, next to the Toy Soldier, represents the 1600s. The second story extends out over the street level floor because taxes in the 1600s were based on the ground floor space and so creative homeowners built structures with larger second floors to save on their tax bills. The 1700s are represented in the "Mini Hyde Park" area by buildings made of plaster and wood. The Georgian-style stone buildings are typical of the 1800s.

Did You Know?

POST-IMPRESSIONIST ARTIST GEORGES SEURAT'S FAMOUS PAINTING, "A SUNDAY AFTERNOON ON THE ISLAND OF LA GRANDE JATTE," INSPIRED THE FRANCE PAVILION'S PARK ALONG THE CANAL NEAR THE INTERNATIONAL GATEWAY.

Did You Know?

THE NORWAY PAVILION IS THE WORLD'S LARGEST NORWEGIAN TOURIST ATTRACTION (NEXT TO NORWAY, OF COURSE), WITH MORE THAN 4.5 MILLION ANNUAL VISITORS — NEARLY THE SAME AS NORWAY'S TOTAL POPULATION.

83. b.) 1988
Located between Mexico and China and sponsored by a group of Norwegian corporations, the Norway pavilion celebrates the history and culture of one of the oldest nations in the West. World Showcase's newest pavilion, it opened May 6, 1988.

84. a.) *King Arthur and the Holy Grail*
A small group of actors known as the World Showcase Players performs a hilarious rendition of the classic tale of King Arthur and the Holy Grail near the UK pavilion, with the help of audience members, who are selected at random to participate.

85. d.) Canada
If you head to the right as you enter World Showcase from Future World, the first pavilion you reach would be Canada. This pavilion features the Hotel du Canada as its icon and includes mountains, gardens, and a 30-foot waterfall!

Did You Know?

THE CONCEPTS FOR THE *HORIZONS* RIDE, WHICH DEPICTED FAMILY LIFE IN THE 21ST CENTURY, WERE DEVELOPED BY TWO CEOS OF GENERAL ELECTRIC, REGINALD JONES AND JACK WELCH, HIS SUCCESSOR.

86. b.) They are designed to look like rooms in a house.
In Germany, the stores are designed to look like rooms in a house. Each room is themed to the merchandise it sells. Wine is sold in the "wine cellar"; food in the wood-floored "kitchen," works of art, out of the "attic"; Christmas decorations in the warm and comfortable "living room." Its Glas und Porzellan shop is one of only eight outlets worldwide to carry a complete collection of Hummel figurines.

87. c.) Morocco
The King of Morocco, who wanted accuracy in every detail of the pavilion, sent 19 Moroccan artists ("maalems") to Florida to install the extensive mosaics you will see throughout this exotic pavilion. The maalems required more than nine tons of handmade enameled terra-cotta tile to complete their mosaic artworks.

88. d.) Philadelphia Orchestra
The half-hour *The American Adventure* show tells the history of America and its people to a moving soundtrack performed by the Philadelphia Orchestra and played over one of the most advanced digital sound systems that Disney has ever used. The attraction's theme song, "Golden Dream," was written by Randy Bright and Bob Moline, arranged and conducted by longtime Disney composer Buddy Baker, and recorded with lead vocals by Richard Page and Marti McCall.

89. d.) China
China's "Monkey King" tells his humorous story from the ancient and classic Chinese folk tale "Journey to the West": how he was born out of stone, became very wise, learned magic, and could transform himself into thousands of shapes and turn somersaults of 18,000 miles each. His story is one of the greatest legends of the East, and virtually every Chinese child knows his tale.

Do You Know?

"BEAUTY AND THE BEAST" – LIVE ON STAGE DEBUTED AT THE STUDIOS' THEATER OF THE STARS ON NOVEMBER 22, 1991, THE SAME DAY THE FEATURE FILM OPENED IN THEATERS, MARKING THE FIRST TIME A STAGE VERSION OF THE FILM THAT INSPIRED IT OPENED ON THE SAME DAY AS THE MOVIE.

CHAPTER FOUR

DISNEY-MGM STUDIOS*

1. What is the official "icon" of Disney-MGM Studios?
- a.) The Earful Tower
- b.) Sorcerer Mickey Hat
- c.) Mann's Chinese Theater
- d.) Crossroads of the World

2. About how many Guests can view each performance of the *Lights, Motors, Action!* stunt show?
- a.) 550
- b.) 1,550
- c.) 5,000
- d.) 7,100

3. What song does Miss Piggy sing in her solo in *Jim Henson's MuppetVision 3-D*?
- a.) "Dream a Little Dream of Me"
- b.) "Somewhere Over the Rainbow"
- c.) "I Just Called to Say I Love You"
- d.) "Unforgettable"

4. On what day of the week did Disney-MGM Studios open?
- a.) Friday
- b.) Saturday
- c.) Sunday
- d.) Monday

5. Who does Minnie Mouse thank next to her hand and footprints outside *The Great Movie Ride*?
- a.) Walt
- b.) Mickey
- c.) Dad
- d.) Everyone

6. What is the name of the dinosaur that's also an ice cream stand?
a.) Gertie
b.) Dino the Diner
c.) Frankie
d.) Diner-Saur

7. About how long is the *Rock 'n' Roller Coaster* ride track?
a.) 1,400 feet
b.) 2,400 feet
c.) 3,400 feet
d.) 4,400 feet

8. What is unique about the suit worn by the James Cagney Audio-Animatronics figure in *The Great Movie Ride*?
a.) It was worn in the movie.
b.) It was donated by his family.
c.) It was originally displayed in Downtown Disney.
d.) It's on loan from Warner Bros.

9. When you "Phone a Complete Stranger" in *Who Wants To Be A Millionaire — Play It*, where is the stranger located?
a.) Mickey Avenue
b.) The Magic Kingdom
c.) Hollywood Boulevard
d.) 50's Prime Time Café

10. What show did *The Hunchback of Notre Dame: A Musical Adventure* replace in 1996?
a.) *Here Come the Muppets*
b.) *Colors of the Wind: Friends from the Animal Forest*
c.) *Spirit of Pocahontas*
d.) *Pocahontas and Her Forest Friends*

11. Who is your navigator on *Star Tours*?
a.) R5-D4
b.) R2-D2
c.) C-3PO
d.) Rex

12. What was Mama Melrose's Ristorante Italiano originally called?

Did You Know?

THE MALEFICENT DRAGON FOR THE *FANTASMIC!* SHOW WEIGHS A MASSIVE 32,000 POUNDS, HAS A 50-FOOT WINGSPAN, AND RISES 50 FEET INTO THE AIR, WHILE THE COBRA THAT JAFAR TRANSFORMS INTO IS 100 FEET LONG AND 16 FEET TALL.

a.) Tony's Pizza and Pasta
b.) Mama Melrose's Kitchen
c.) Aunt Millie's Café
d.) The Studio Pizzeria

13. How was the Studios' giant water tower modified in 1995 to honor a Florida sports team?
    a.) A Florida Marlins hat was added
    b.) A Miami Dolphins logo was added
    c.) A pair of protective goggles was added
    d.) A Mighty Ducks hockey mask was painted on it

14. What is the brand and model of the very large guitar seen at *Rock 'n' Roller Coaster's* entrance?
    a.) Fender Stratocaster
    b.) Gibson Les Paul

c.) G-Force Acoustic
d.) Mousegetar

15. Female "gangsters" weren't seen on *The Great Movie Ride* until ___?
    a.) 1990
    b.) 1995
    c.) 2000
    d.) 2003

16. What is the name of the 3-D character created in *Jim Henson's MuppetVision 3-D*?
    a.) Sweetums
    b.) Waldorf
    c.) Beaker
    d.) Waldo

17. Near which body of water can you find a dinosaur in the Studios?
    a.) Echo Lake

b.) Hollywood Lagoon
c.) Backlot Bay
d.) Hollywood Hills Bay

18. *Voyage of the Little Mermaid* once starred a former ___?
a.) Miss America
b.) Mr. Universe

c.) Olympic Gold Medalist
d.) Academy Award Winner

19. Who sponsored the now-defunct *Monster Sound Show*?
a.) Kodak
b.) Sony
c.) RCA
d.) G-Force Records

20. Which of these Disney animated features has not had its own parade at the Studios?
a.) *Hercules*
b.) *Mulan*
c.) *Toy Story*
d.) *The Lion King*

21. What's the last "scene" you go through on *The Great Movie Ride*?
a.) *Casablanca*

b.) *Wizard of Oz*
c.) *Raiders of the Lost Ark*
d.) *Aliens*

22. Who is the manufacturer of the TV sets in the 50's Prime Time Café?
a.) GE
b.) RCA
c.) Disney
d.) WED Enterprises

23. What show did *Voyage of the Little Mermaid* replace?
a.) *Here Come the Muppets*
b.) *Bear in the Big Blue House*
c.) *SuperStar Television*
d.) *Doug Live!*

24. In *The Twilight Zone Tower of Terror*, what time did lightning strike, stopping the hotel's clocks?
a.) 5:55 PM
b.) 8:05 PM
c.) 9:35 AM
d.) 11:55 PM

25. Which of these *Star Wars* characters cannot be seen in *Star Tours*?
a.) Admiral Ackbar
b.) R2-D2
c.) A Jawa
d.) C-3PO

26. What's the first Audio-Animatronics movie scene you encounter on *The Great Movie Ride*?
a.) *Footlight Parade*
b.) *Singin' in the Rain*

c.) *Mary Poppins*
d.) *Casablanca*

27. In *MuppetVision 3-D*, Waldo says "They'll never recognize me now!" He then transforms himself into what character?
a.) Mickey
b.) Goofy
c.) Kermit
d.) Stitch

28. What talk show host could be found in the former *SuperStar Television* attraction?
a.) David Letterman
b.) Jay Leno

c.) Rosie O' Donnell
d.) Johnny Carson

29. How many seconds does it take you to reach 60 mph in the beginning of *Rock 'n' Roller Coaster Starring Aerosmith*?
a.) 1.5
b.) 4.1
c.) 2.8
d.) The top speed is 57 mph.

30. What is the name of the "cleaning lady" who sometimes entertains the audience before the *Indiana Jones Epic Stunt Spectacular* begins?

Did You Know?

IN *DISNEY-MGM STUDIOS BACKLOT TOUR*, THE AIR CANNONS USED TO SHOOT THE WATER IN CATASTROPHE CANYON ARE SO POWERFUL THAT THEY COULD BLAST A BASKETBALL OVER THE EMPIRE STATE BUILDING. IN FACT, THE JETS SHOOT OUT ENOUGH WATER TO FILL 10 OLYMPIC-SIZE SWIMMING POOLS IN JUST A FEW SECONDS!

a.) Helga
b.) Rosie
c.) Betty
d.) Marilyn

31. In _Disney-MGM Studios Backlot Tour_, what company name will you find on the oil tanker in Catastrophe Canyon?
a.) Mojave Oil Company
b.) Tetak Oil Company
c.) Harambe Oil Co.
d.) Big Thunder Oil Company

32. What is the destination of each trip taken on _Star Tours_?
a.) Hoth
b.) Tatooine
c.) The Death Star
d.) Moon of Endor

33. Which of these films is not represented in _The Great Movie Ride_ in either a 3-D or ride-through scene?

a.) _Footlight Parade_
b.) _The Public Enemy_
c.) _Star Wars_
d.) _Raiders of the Lost Ark_

34. The space occupied by _Playhouse Disney – Live on Stage!_ was once home to ___?
a.) Soundstage Restaurant
b.) _Doug Live!_
c.) _Hunchback of Notre Dame: A Musical Adventure_
d.) The _Spirit of Pocahontas_ show

35. What is the name of the hotel featured in _The Twilight Zone Tower of Terror_?
a.) Hollywood Hills Hotel
b.) Hollywood Hotel
c.) Beverly Hills Hotel
d.) Hollywood Tower Hotel

36. Who was the original sponsor of _Star Tours_?
a.) Kenner

Did You Know?

THE FENDER STRATOCASTER GUITAR OUTSIDE THE _ROCK 'N' ROLLER COASTER_ IS 15 TIMES NORMAL SIZE.

b.) Mattel
c.) Energizer
d.) M&M Mars

37. What happens at the end of "Beauty and the Beast" – Live on Stage?
a.) Balloons are released.
b.) The Cast comes into the audience to shake hands.
c.) White doves are released.
d.) Rose petals drop from the ceiling.

38. Who hosted the opening of the Studios in 1989?
a.) Robin Williams
b.) John Ritter
c.) Mickey Rooney
d.) Harry Anderson

39. Drew Carey's character in Sounds Dangerous was named after a character in what classic film?
a.) *The Godfather*
b.) *Gone with the Wind*
c.) *A Streetcar Named Desire*
d.) *Citizen Kane*

40. When the Rock 'n' Roller Coaster had its first anniversary, WDW celebrated it by ___?
a.) Staging a free, unannounced concert by Aerosmith
b.) Building a Stratocaster in the parking lot made out of Chevrolet Corvettes
c.) Turning on the lights inside the ride at random intervals
d.) Increasing its speed by 5 mph

Did You Know?

THE AMOUNT OF PAINT USED TO COVER THE SORCERER MICKEY HAT IN DISNEY-MGM STUDIOS COULD COVER 500 CADILLAC AUTOMOBILES!

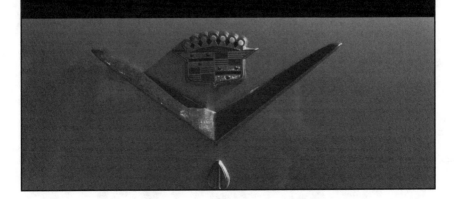

41. The gift shop at the exit of *Star Tours* is currently called ___?
a.) The Death Star Gift Shop
b.) Endor Vendors
c.) Tatooine Traders
d.) Star Traders

42. What is smuggled by Lefty Moreno in *Sounds Dangerous*?
a.) Diamonds
b.) Snowglobes
c.) Gold
d.) The Mona Lisa

43. Which of the following was NOT planned for the Studios?
a.) *Baby Herman's Runaway Buggy Ride*
b.) *Dick Tracy's Crimestoppers Ride*
c.) *A Muppet Movie Ride*
d.) *Pocahontas Indian Village*

44. What is the name of the record company featured in *Rock 'n' Roller Coaster*?
a.) WED Studios
b.) G-Force Records
c.) Disney Studios
d.) Buena Vista Records

45. You find yourself on what street when you enter the Studios?
a.) Sunset Boulevard
b.) Hollywood Boulevard
c.) Mickey Avenue
d.) Studio Street

46. What powers each stunt car in the *Lights, Motors, Action!* show?
a.) A motorcycle engine
b.) A 300 hp racer engine
c.) A diesel-powered rotary engine
d.) A clean-burning ethanol race-car engine

47. In *Star Tours*, who provides the voice for your rookie robot StarSpeeder 3000 pilot?
a.) Billy Crystal
b.) Anthony Daniels (the voice of C-3PO)
c.) Paul Reubens
d.) Robin Williams

THE ANSWERS
TO CHAPTER FOUR

1. b.) Sorcerer Mickey hat
Disney erected the 122-foot Sorcerer Mickey Hat in front of Mann's Chinese Theater in 2001 as part of its "100 Years of Magic Celebration" honoring Walt Disney's hundredth birthday and creative legacy. The 156-ton hat replaced the Studios' Earful Tower (that's the large water tower with Mickey ears) as the park's icon, filling the same function for the Studios that Cinderella Castle fills for the Magic Kingdom.

2. c.) 5,000
Lights, Motors, Action! Extreme Stunt Show, inspired by a similar show in Disneyland Paris, takes place in a 6.5-acre area, around a Mediterranean-themed set, and includes a vehicle garage and a 5,000-seat stadium. The arena sits in an area that was formerly home to what was known as "Residential Avenue."

3. a.) "Dream a Little Dream of Me"
Miss Piggy's solo in *MuppetVision 3-D* is ruined when Bean Bunny tries to spice up her act a bit by adding his own 3-D effects. Reach out and pop one of the real bubbles falling from the ceiling during her performance.

4. d.) Monday
The Studios opened on a rainy Monday, May 1, 1989. It got lots of press coverage, including an NBC-TV two-hour special — *Night of*

Stars, Spectacle and Excitement. The show included a walk-through tour of the park for viewers.

5. d.) Everyone
Minnie followed in the long Hollywood tradition of putting her hand and foot (paw?) prints in the cement outside the replica of Mann's Chinese Theater. Her prints are dated 5/1/89, the Studios' opening day.

6. a.) Gertie
Gertie was affectionately named after vaudeville artist and actor Winsor McCay's animated dinosaur. Created in about 1912, McCay's "Gertie" was the first animated character to show emotion, as well as the silver screen's first dinosaur. McCay drew about 14,000 frames of Gertie and background scenery on rice paper, and began showing this first projected cartoon to audiences around 1915. Walt Disney met McCay's son years later, and told him he owed much of his inspiration as an animator to McCay.

7. c.) 3,400 feet
The 3,403 feet of track in the 3.7 million cubic foot *Rock 'n' Roller Coaster Starring Aerosmith* show building takes Guests through three inversions — two rollover loops and one corkscrew. It takes each "limo" 3.12 minutes to go from start to finish, coincidentally the exact running time of one of Aerosmith's

Greatest Hits, "Sweet Emotion."

8. b.) It was donated by his family.
Although the tuxedo worn by the Cagney Audio-Animatronics figure in *The Great Movie Ride* was once owned by James Cagney, it was never used in a film. In fact, the style of the tux does not even match the period of *The Public Enemy,* the Cagney film featured in this ride.

9. a.) Mickey Avenue
The "lifelines" available to players in WDW's "Hot Seat" are the 50/50, "Ask the Audience," and a slightly different "Phone a Friend" option. Rather than allowing Guests to call a friend who might not be home (and to avoid those long-distance calls overseas), players can "Phone a Complete Stranger." If the contestant chooses this lifeline, a phone rings near the entrance to the Millionaire Soundstage on Mickey

Avenue. A waiting Cast Member then hands the phone at random to a Guest who is passing by.

10. c.) *Spirit of Pocahontas*

Spirit of Pocahontas was performed in the Backlot Theater beginning in 1995 to coincide with the release of the Disney animated film, *Pocahontas*. The production took you to a forest in Virginia, where a Powhatan storyteller named Werowance told the story of John Smith and Pocahontas in the shadow of a 28-foot Grandmother Willow puppet. The show closed February 24, 1996, and was replaced by *Hunchback of Notre Dame: A Musical Adventure*. Pocahontas returned to WDW in 1998, when a show called *Colors of the Wind: Friends from the Animal Forest* (later *Pocahontas and Her Forest Friends*) opened in Camp Minnie-Mickey in Disney's Animal Kingdom. *Here Come the Muppets* was located at the end of the walking portion of *The Backstage Studio Tour*.

11. b.) R2-D2

R2-D2 is your capable navigator — fortunately, because you'll need his help to get out of the mess your pilot, Rex, gets you into!

12. d.) The Studio Pizzeria

This restaurant opened on June 15, 1991, and closed three months later.

13. c.) A pair of protective goggles was added

Blue goggles, similar to those worn by star Horace Grant, were placed on the Studios' water tower in 1995 to celebrate the Orlando Magic's NBA playoff appearance. The Magic made it to the finals, but eventually lost.

14. a.) Fender Stratocaster

Guests line up in the shadows of a 40-foot tall, red Fender Stratocaster outside the *Rock 'n' Roller Coaster*. The Stratocaster is exact in almost every detail, except that it's gigantic — 15 times normal size, giving it a 32-foot-long neck.

15. c.) 2000

Only male Cast Members played gangsters during the live-action sequence for *The Great Movie Ride*'s first 11 years. "Mugsi Tocatta," the first female gangster, joined in 2000.

16. d.) Waldo

Dr. Bunsen Honeydew and his assistant, Beaker, create "Waldo," the Spirit of 3-D, in an experiment

Did You Know?

THE EARS ON THE GIANT (YET EMPTY)
DISNEY-MGM STUDIOS WATER TOWER ARE
HAT SIZE 342 3/8, WEIGH 2.5 TONS, AND
ARE SOMETIMES DECORATED TO CELEBRATE
SPECIAL EVENTS AND THE HOLIDAYS.

gone wrong in *Jim Henson's Muppet-Vision 3-D*. Waldorf is the name of one of the grumpy old hecklers in the balcony.

17. a.) Echo Lake
Dinosaur Gertie serves "Ice Cream of Extinction" on the shores of Echo Lake. You can get cones, bars, or ice cream sandwiches.

18. a.) Miss America
Crowned Miss America in 1993, Leanza Cornett was the first Miss Florida to win the Miss America title. She has appeared as a reporter on *Entertainment Tonight*, co-hosted numerous shows including Lifetime Network's *New Attitudes*, and also starred in *Barefoot in the Park*.

19. b.) Sony
The *Monster Sound Show*, presented by Sony, was one of the Studios' opening day attractions. It was later replaced by the *ABC Sound Show*.

20. d.) *The Lion King*
The Lion King has not had its own Disney-MGM Studios parade. There is a *Festival of the Lion King* show at Disney's Animal Kingdom, however, and there used to be a *Legend of the Lion King* attraction in the Magic Kingdom's Fantasyland.

21. b.) *Wizard of Oz*
Following the Munchkinland scene in *The Great Movie Ride*, Guests are treated to a grand finale in the form of a memorable film montage that includes some of the greatest scenes and lines in movie history.

22. c.) Disney
Travel back to the 1950s for some home-cooked meals in this wonderfully themed restaurant. Wait in the living room for your table in Mom's

kitchen. Take a look at every detail that surrounds you — Formica counters, cow-shaped salt and pepper shakers, and even the "Disney" TVs showing clips of old shows. A true dining "experience." Try the meatloaf! At least 125 orders of meatloaf and mashed potatoes are requested every single day at the 50's Prime Time Café!

23. a.) *Here Come the Muppets*

Here Come the Muppets was a temporary show that ran while *Muppet-Vision 3-D* was being built. It included performances by Kermit, Miss Piggy, and Fozzie Bear, as well as Dr. Teeth and the Electric Mayhem band, which crashed a red "monorail" on stage as their entrance.

24. b.) 8:05 PM

At exactly 8:05 PM on Halloween night, 1939, the hotel was struck by lightning, causing all of the clocks to stop at that time and five unfortunate riders of the elevator to be lost to . . . the Twilight Zone.

25. c.) A Jawa

Those lovable droids, C-3PO and R2-D2, can be seen in the *Star Tours* queue area, near the model of the StarSpeeder. Can't find Admiral Ackbar? (Or don't know who he is?) Look in the control tower! He's the orange guy who looks like he's got big fish eyes.

26. b.) *Singin' in the Rain*

Gene Kelly's Audio-Animatronics figure is the first operating AA figure you meet in *The Great Movie Ride*.

27. a.) Mickey

The world's first "digitized puppet," Waldo C. Graphic, was originally created in 1989 for *The Jim Henson Hour*. Waldo was created by Kirk Thatcher of Pacific Data Images and played by Steve Whitmire.

28. d.) Johnny Carson

Through the use of "blue screen technology," *SuperStar Television* allowed Guests to take part in some of television's most famous moments. Volunteers were chosen to "appear" in such classic TV shows as *I Love Lucy, The Golden Girls, Cheers,*

Did You Know?

THE TWO MARBLE DOORS YOU SEE AS YOU ENTER
THE QUEUE AREA FOR *ROCK 'N' ROLLER COASTER* ARE
EACH DECORATED WITH 3,536 MULTICOLORED MARBLES.
YUP. THE KIND YOU USED TO SHOOT
WHEN YOU WERE A KID.

Empty Nest, and *Gilligan's Island*. *Doug Live!* replaced this show, which was sponsored by Sony, in the spring of 1999.

29. c.) 2.8 seconds
Not only do you go from 0 to 60 mph in 2.8 seconds, but you will experience 5 Gs of force as you go into the first loop of *Rock 'n' Roller Coaster*. What does that really mean? How about this: the liftoff of NASA's Space Shuttle subjects astronauts to 3 Gs of force.

30. b.) Rosie
As Guests enter the theater for the *Indiana Jones* stunt show, they are often entertained by Francis the plumber or Rosie, a "cleaning lady" who is both loud and funny.

31. a.) Mojave Oil Company
You can also see a reference to Mojave Oil Company on the gas pumps at Oscar's Super Service Station, located at the entrance to the park. Oscar's doesn't sell any gas;

instead, it rents strollers and lockers.

32. d.) Moon of Endor
Guests can travel in a 40-passenger StarSpeeder 3000 to the peaceful moon of Endor. Piece of cake, right? Well, your routine trip quickly becomes a fast-paced adventure through meteor showers, and smack dab into the middle of a Rebel battle with the Empire. Maybe you should hold on . . . ummm . . . tight. May the Force be with you.

33. c.) *Star Wars*
Among the films represented in *The Great Movie Ride* are *Footlight Parade*, *The Public Enemy*, *Singin' in the Rain*, *The Wizard of Oz*, *Mary Poppins*, *The Man With No Name*, *Alien*, *Raiders of the Lost Ark*, *Tarzan*, and *Casablanca*.

34. a.) Soundstage Restaurant
Prior to becoming a performance space, the area where *Playhouse Disney* now plays housed a restaurant. The Soundstage opened with the Studios and was designed to look

like a "wrap party" for the film *Big Business*, with Cast Members costumed to look like they worked for a studio catering company. Over time, the restaurant's theme changed to spotlight Disney's animated film releases.

35. d.) Hollywood Tower Hotel

The Hollywood Tower Hotel was inspired in part by three famous California hotels: The Mission Inn in Riverside, the Biltmore in Los Angeles, and the Chateau Marmont in Hollywood. As a Guest there, you may want to take the stairs when going to your room. They seem to be experiencing a few minor glitches with the elevator system.

36. d.) M&M Mars

Star Tours was sponsored by candy giant M&M Mars, prior to being presented by Energizer (the pink bunny people). What Mars had to do with *Star Wars*, I'll never know. (And I can neither confirm nor deny the rumor that Disney was going to allow it to sponsor *Spaceship Earth* for the Millennium Celebration and turn it into a giant M&M.)

37. c.) White doves are released.

White doves are released and onstage fireworks are ignited at the glorious conclusion of the Broadway-quality

show, *"Beauty and the Beast" – Live on Stage*.

38. b.) John Ritter
The late John Ritter hosted the Studios' Grand Opening, which was featured in a celebrity-packed special on NBC-TV.

39. d.) *Citizen Kane*
Drew Carey's character in *Sounds Dangerous* is named "Charlie Foster," a tribute to the title character from *Citizen Kane*, Charles Foster Kane.

40. b.) Building a Stratocaster in the parking lot made out of Chevrolet Corvettes
To commemorate the first anniversary of the opening of *Rock 'n' Roller Coaster*, Disney built a giant replica of a Fender Stratocaster guitar in the parking lot — out of Corvettes! More than 80 Chevrolet Corvettes, of various years and models, but all red, black or white, were arranged

to create the design, which was only visible from above.

41. c.) Tatooine Traders
The original *Star Tours* shop was called Endor Vendors, but the name was changed to Tatooine Traders in late 1999 to coincide with the release of *Star Wars: Episode I*.

42. a.) Diamonds
Bumbling detective Charlie Foster accidentally discovers that the Snowglobe Company he has infiltrated is just a front for a diamond-

smuggling operation. And yes, the observant Guest can see that he bumps into a Snowglobe employee carrying what appears to be the Mona Lisa at the beginning of the film.

43. d.) *Pocahontas Indian Village*
Problems after Jim Henson's death led to the cancellation of a Muppets ride similar to *The Great Movie Ride*. *Baby Herman's Runaway Buggy Ride*, based on the *Who Framed Roger Rabbit?* film, was planned for a "Maroon Studios" area that never came to pass. And it was most likely

disappointing box office results that led to the scrapping of a *Dick Tracy's Crimestoppers Ride*.

44. b.) G-Force Records

Rock 'n' Roller Coaster begins with a walking tour of the fictional G-Force Records company. Then you meet up with the rock band Aerosmith, and that's when things REALLY get fun! (This ain't no Barry Manilow concert you're going to!)

45. b.) Hollywood Boulevard

The boulevard, lined with Disney memorabilia shops, is a re-creation of Tinsel Town during its glamorous heyday in the 1930s. It is adorned with '30s architecture, such as the Keystone Clothiers building, which is partially patterned after Hollywood's famous Max Factor building.

46. a.) A motorcycle engine

The amazing red and black stunt cars used in *Lights, Motors, Action!* were custom built. Each is powered by a 1300cc motorcycle engine, mounted behind the driver's seat for optimal weight distribution.

47. c.) Paul Reubens

Better known for his role as PeeWee Herman, Paul Reubens isn't at all what Disney Imagineers originally had in mind to pilot the StarSpeeder tour. They had imagined a robotic veteran of the Clone Wars, but George Lucas wanted a rookie pilot instead.

Did You Know?

THE OASIS GARDENS IN THE OASIS WERE
ORIGINALLY GOING TO BE CALLED
"GENESIS GARDENS," BUT DISNEY DECIDED
THAT THE RELIGIOUS CONNOTATION OF "GENESIS"
MIGHT PROVE TOO CONTROVERSIAL.

CHAPTER FIVE

Disney's Animal Kingdom

1. Disney spends more than $1,700,000 yearly on what for Disney's Animal Kingdom (DAK)?
- a.) Worms
- b.) Manure
- c.) Airline tickets to import new animals from overseas
- d.) Plant food

2. The baobab trees on the *Kilimanjaro Safaris* are ___?
- a.) Really from Africa
- b.) Camouflaged animal feeders

- c.) Made out of fiberglass and steel
- d.) Known biologically as *Disneyodendron eximius*

3. *Tarzan Rocks!* was located in what Animal Kingdom venue?
- a.) Theater in the Wild
- b.) Caravan Stage
- c.) Discovery Island Theater
- d.) DinoLand Theater

4. Who portrays Dr. Grant Seeker in *DINOSAUR?*

THE WALT DISNEY WORLD TRIVIA BOOK

a.) Phylicia Rashad
b.) Wallace Langham
c.) Bill Nye, the Science Guy
d.) Eric Idle

5. What is unique about the *Wildlife Express Train* to Rafiki's Planet Watch?
   a.) It runs on electricity.
   b.) It was recovered in Mexico and refurbished by Disney Imagineers.
   c.) Its passengers sit sideways.
   d.) It was originally part of the *WDW Railroad* line in the Magic Kingdom.

6. Which of the following about *Expedition Everest* is true?
   a.) The ride travels forwards and backwards.
   b.) The "mountain" is the tallest in Florida.
   c.) The ride vehicles are known as "Steam Donkeys."
   d.) All of the above.

7. As you enter Disney's Animal Kingdom, what is the first land that you reach?
   a.) Africa
   b.) Discovery Island
   c.) The Oasis
   d.) Harambe Village

8. About how many branches are on *The Tree of Life*?
   a.) 500
   b.) 1,000
   c.) 3,000
   d.) 8,000

9. What fictitious highway runs through Chester & Hester's Dino-Rama!?
   a.) Oldengate Parkway
   b.) Dinosaurus Drive
   c.) Boneyard Boulevard
   d.) Diggs County Highway

10. DAK has the largest collection of what in North America?
   a.) Flowering trees
   b.) Giraffes
   c.) Animal keepers
   d.) Sprinkler heads

11. Which of these DAK theaters holds the greatest number of Guests?
   a.) Caravan Stage
   b.) Theater in the Wild
   c.) Grandmother Willow's Grove
   d.) Lion King Theater

Did You Know?

60 DUMP TRUCKS FULL OF DIRT WERE DELIVERED TO THE DAK CONSTRUCTION SITE EVERY DAY FOR 2 YEARS STRAIGHT TO CREATE THE PARK'S LANDSCAPE. THAT'S ABOUT 4.4 MILLION CUBIC YARDS OF DIRT.

12. What are Cast Members in Camp Minnie-Mickey supposed to be?

- a.) Residents of the Adirondack Mountains
- b.) Stranded survivors of a plane crash
- c.) Camp counselors
- d.) Zookeepers

13. You tour five different habitats on the *Kilimanjaro Safaris* ride. Which of these is NOT one of them?

- a.) East Savanna
- b.) Savanna Flamingo Pool
- c.) Pangani Forest
- d.) Ituri Forest

Did You Know?

WHILE DISNEY'S ANIMAL KINGDOM (DAK) INCLUDES PLANTS FROM EVERY CONTINENT ON EARTH EXCEPT ANTARCTICA, THE FIRST TREE PLANTED ON THE DAK SITE, IN DECEMBER 1995, WAS AN *ACACIA XANTHOPHLOEA*, GROWN FROM A SEED WHICH LEAD CREATIVE DESIGNER AND PRINCIPLE LANDSCAPE ARCHITECT PAUL COMSTOCK ACQUIRED IN AFRICA.

14. What modified structure was used as the basis for DAK's icon, *The Tree of Life*?
- a.) An oil rig
- b.) Elements from the old *Horizons* attraction in Epcot
- c.) A water tower
- d.) Pylons used to support the monorail beams

15. Where would you find a "Darting Dragonfly" and a "Leaping Lizard"?
- a.) *Pangani Forest Expedition Trail*
- b.) *Discovery River Boats*

- c.) Rafiki's Planet Watch
- d.) *Festival of the Lion King*

16. What is the name of the dinosaur that interacted with DAK Guests in 2005 and is the first ever free-moving Audio-Animatronics figure?
- a.) Jiminy
- b.) Sue
- c.) Barney
- d.) Lucky

17. The original concept for DAK divided the park into three distinct areas focusing on ___?

a.) Conservation, a zoo, and animal research

b.) Animals from the land, sea, and air

c.) Real, mythical, and extinct animals

d.) Exploration, archaeology, and the environment

18. Who is the proprietor of the Muziki, a musical instrument "shop" in Africa?

a.) Chief Nammie

b.) R. Ongala

c.) M. Ziwani

d.) Tamu Tamu

19. What is the motto of the tour company in *Expedition Everest*?

a.) "There and Back with the Flying Yak"

b.) "Ain't No Mountain High Enough"

c.) "Wild By Design"

d.) "Trust Us"

20. Who is "Mr. Imagination"?

a.) The creator of the Time Rover

b.) The original proprietor of Chester & Hester's Dino-Rama!

c.) Your host of *Conservation Station*

d.) The sculptor of a dinosaur statue in DinoLand U.S.A.

21. What animal was "mistakenly" almost left off *The Tree of Life*?

a.) Dragon
b.) Elephant
c.) Mouse
d.) Chimpanzee

22. How do you say "Place of Enchantment" in Swahili?
a.) Anandapur
b.) Pangani
c.) Rafiki
d.) Harambe

23. What is the name of the mountain you travel through in DAK's newest thrill ride?
a.) Mount Everest
b.) Serka Zong
c.) Forbidden Mountain
d.) Mount Kilimanjaro

24. Who is the host for the 3-D film, *It's Tough to be a Bug!*?
a.) Flik
b.) Hopper
c.) Ellen Degeneres
d.) Chili

25. What land in DAK has the greatest number of attractions?
a.) Africa
b.) DinoLand U.S.A.
c.) Asia
d.) Rafiki's Planet Watch

26. On which attraction do you enter the Anandapur Royal Forest?
a.) *Kilimanjaro Safaris*
b.) *Kali River Rapids*

Did You Know?

THE FASTPASS AND THE STANDBY LINES IN EXPEDITION EVEREST ARE THEMED DIFFERENTLY, AS IT IS ASSUMED, EVEN WITHIN THE STORY, THAT YOU ARE ON A "FAST TRACK" TO GET THROUGH AND THEREFORE BYPASS THE BOOKING OFFICE. IN EITHER LINE, YOU WILL HAVE AN OPPORTUNITY TO "PURCHASE SUPPLIES" BEFORE YOU BOARD THE TRAIN AND YOUR JOURNEY BEGINS.

c.) *Wildlife Express Train*

d.) *Maharajah Jungle Trek*

27. How many stories (not feet) high is *The Tree of Life*?

a.) 4

b.) 14

c.) 34

d.) 44

28. Who did Disney collaborate with when designing *Expedition Everest*?

a.) The SciFi Channel

b.) The U.S. Government

c.) The Discovery Network

d.) The Yeti's cousin, Bigfoot

29. What is the name of the parade seen in DAK during the holiday season?

a.) *Festival of the Holidays*

b.) *Mickey's Jammin' Jungle Parade*

c.) *Share a Dream Come True*

d.) *Mickey's Jingle Jungle Parade*

30. Which of the following shares its name with an attraction that was initially conceived for DAK's proposed land celebrating mythical creatures?

a.) *Expedition Everest*

b.) Fantasia Gardens

c.) *Tower of Terror*

d.) Dinosaur Gertie's Ice Cream of Extinction

31. What is the name of the fictional village found at the base of the *Expedition Everest* mountain?

a.) Serka Zong

b.) Rhodesia

Did You Know?

IT TOOK MORE THAN 5 MONTHS AND OVER 120 ARTISTS TO CREATE THE 4 MURALS THAT HONOR THE PAST RULERS OF THE FICTIONAL VILLAGE OF ANANDAPUR.

c.) The Forbidden City
d.) Nepal

32. According to Grandmother Willow, only who can save the forest?
a.) Pocahontas
b.) Pocahontas's forest friends
c.) Humans
d.) Disney Imagineers

33. What color are the dinosaur ride vehicles in *TriceraTop Spin*?
a.) Brown
b.) Gray
c.) Pink
d.) Green

34. What was the original design for DAK's central icon?
a.) A merry-go-round
b.) A giant aviary
c.) A mountain roller coaster
d.) A 90-foot aquarium tower

35. Which attraction was the first to open in the Asia section of Animal Kingdom?
a.) *Kali River Rapids*
b.) *Maharajah Jungle Trek*
c.) *Flights of Wonder*
d.) *Discovery River Boats*

36. What is the slogan of the *Kilimanjaro Safaris*?
a.) "When it comes to Safaris, we go WILD!"
b.) "Nahtazu!"
c.) "It's just like being there — because you ARE!"
d.) "True Life Adventures in the African Wild"

37. What are the ride vehicles in *DINOSAUR* called?
a.) Doom Buggies
b.) Time Rovers
c.) XP-37s
d.) Zulu 174s

The Answers
TO CHAPTER FIVE

1. a.) Worms
Yeah, that's right. Disney spends more than $1.7 million per year on worms to feed many of the park's inhabitants. Want fries with that?

2. b.) Camouflaged animal feeders
Seven of the nine baobab trees on the *Kilimanjaro Safaris* are made of concrete and are both practical and part of the "show." They act as feeders for the animals, and also house

horticultural equipment. Some contain "lazy susans" that rotate hourly to feed giraffes willow and acacia shoots. Others contain hidden surveillance cameras. The only live baobab tree is in Harambe outside the Tusker House restaurant.

3. a.) Theater in the Wild
The hexagonal, roofed theater closed January 21, 2006, for refurbishment. When it reopens, it will be fully enclosed (instead of just covered), air-conditioned, and home to a new show that will succeed the high-energy *Tarzan Rocks!* production, which included performances by singers, dancers, acrobatic monkeys, giraffes, and even in-line skaters!

4. b.) Wallace Langham
You may recognize Wallace Langham from his role in TV's *Veronica's Closet* and from his small role in the 1980s teen movie *Weird Science*. Dr. Seeker is the scientist who tells you that your trip back in time is not only to observe but also to bring back a particular dinosaur before the species is rendered extinct by a meteor heading towards Earth!

6. d.) All of the above.
Expedition Everest, Disney's newest and one of its most-anticipated attractions in years, opened in Asia in April 2006. Almost 200 feet high, the man-made superstructure for the ride is Florida's highest "mountain." Inside, trains known as "Steam Donkeys" take Guests forward and backward through canyons and caverns in search of the mysterious Yeti.

7. c.) The Oasis
As you pass through DAK's gates, you encounter The Oasis, a lush tropical land filled with exotic birds, animals, and plants. Although there are no attractions here, you can meander through the crisscrossing pathways and look for iguanas, birds, turtles, and other wildlife before crossing onto Discovery Island, from which you can reach every other land in the park.

8 d.) 8,000
Imagineers considered *The Tree of Life* the single most challenging structure on property. More than 103,000 leaves — all attached by hand and capable of withstanding 100 mph winds — adorn the tree's more than 8,000 branches and its leaves stretch out more than 160 feet at its widest part.

9. d.) Diggs County Highway
Signs for travelers passing through Chester & Hester's Dino-Rama!

5. c.) Its passengers sit sideways.
The cars on this replica of a pastoral African train are designed to give Guests the best possible view of the savannah and backstage parts of the park as *Wildlife Express* travels to DAK's conservation area. Guests sit in two tiered rows of seats facing the open left side of the car.

let Guests know that they are on Diggs County Highway, Route 498. (Disney's Animal Kingdom opened in 4/98 — April 1998.)

10. a.) Flowering trees

About 100,000 trees and 2.5 million individual grass plants were planted when Disney's Animal Kingdom was built. The park also has several specialized plant collections, including the largest collection of African species outside of Africa and the third largest cycad (fern-like plants) collection in the United States. Oh, and by the way, DAK has about 15,000 computer-controlled sprinkler heads to deliver water to the landscape.

11. b.) Theater in the Wild

The DAK theaters range from intimate to quite large. Here's how they rank, from smallest to largest, along with where you will find them and the attractions they currently house (or had last housed as we go to press):
• 350-seat Grandmother Willow's Grove in Camp Minnie-Mickey (*Pocahontas and Her Forest Friends*)
• 1,000-seat Caravan Stage in Asia (*Flights of Wonder*)
• 1,375-seat Lion King Theater in Camp Minnie-Mickey (*Festival of the Lion King*)
• 1,500-seat Theater in the Wild in DinoLand U.S.A. (*Tarzan Rocks!* ran there from July 1999 to January 21, 2006.)

12. c.) Camp counselors

Want to have some extra, improvisational fun next time you visit DAK? Be sure to ask Cast Members where they are from. Why? Because (other than those in Rafiki's Planet Watch), CMs often develop stories (called "niches") about how and why they are living and working in their respective lands. You may hear wild tales about how they came to be villagers in Africa, students at the Dino Institute, or washed ashore at Harambe after being lost at sea. Some may even show you a second-story window in one of the buildings and describe "their room."

13. c.) Pangani Forest

The five habitats on the *Kilimanjaro Safaris* ride are the Ituri Forest, Safi River, West Savanna, Savanna Flamingo Pool, and East Savanna.

14. a.) An oil rig

The Tree of Life is made primarily of concrete, which was fashioned over a modified oil rig for strength and stability. Imagineers hired an oil field contractor in Houston, Texas, to modify an oil rig for the massive tree's frame. The six-legged rig was shipped to DAK in pieces and reassembled by crane.

15. b.) *Discovery River Boats*

The five boats on this short-lived, many-named attraction were: the *Darting Dragonfly, Otter Nonsense,* *Leaping Lizard, Crocodile Belle,* and the *Hasty Hippo.* The ride lasted just 16 months because it was slow loading and combined long lines with a boring round-trip excursion from what was then known as Safari Village (now Discovery Island) to the Upcountry Landing dock in Asia and back. (You could not take a boat from Safari Village to Asia, or vice versa; you had to stay on for the round-trip.)

16. d.) Lucky

As a part of the Happiest Celebration on Earth, Lucky, the first free-moving Audio-Animatronics figure, debuted in DinoLand U.S.A., appearing there from May 5, 2005, through July 28, 2005. He is 9 feet tall, weighs 450 pounds, and can sniffle, burp, hiccup, sneeze, yawn, cough, giggle, snort, purr, and talk.

17. c.) Real, mythical, and extinct animals

Announced on June 20, 1995, by Michael Eisner, Disney's Animal

Kingdom was to take Guests on adventures through a region filled with real animals, a second world filled with mythical creatures such as unicorns, and a third focusing on dinosaurs and other extinct creatures.

18. b.) R. Ongala
Situated along the Discovery River in Africa, Muziki is home to performances by traditional African musicians and singers. The "store" is owned by R. Ongala, whose name can be seen in the signage.

19. a.) "There and Back with the Flying Yak"
The doorway to the entrance to the FASTPASS queue on *Expedition Everest* bears the red sign of the Himalayan Escapes Tour & Expeditions Company, whose mascot, the winged yak, ties in with the company's slogan. "Trust Us" is from the "Cap'n Bob's Super Safaris" signs you can see posted throughout Harambe in the Africa section of the park.

20. d.) The sculptor of a dinosaur statue in DinoLand U.S.A.
Gregory Warmack, better known as Mr. Imagination, is a self-taught artist whose works are primarily made from "junk" — common materials, rubble, and discarded items. He has created a number of works on commission, including pieces for Coca-Cola, The House of Blues, and Disney. You'll find two in WDW:

the bluish dinosaur sculpture with embedded objects outside of Chester & Hester's, and the "Unity Grotto" entranceway arch to the Downtown Disney House of Blues' "Voo-doo Garden."

21. d.) Chimpanzee
The Tree of Life had 324 animal carvings on it and was nearing completion when Jane Goodall inspected it at Disney's invitation. Goodall, considered the world's foremost authority on chimpanzees (she lived in their environment for more than two decades), immediately noticed there was no chimp image. Disney's Imagineers quickly remedied that, adding the likeness of "David Graybeard," one of Goodall's favorite chimps. You can spot him near the entrance of *It's Tough to be a Bug!*

22. b.) Pangani
Pangani Forest Exploration Trail takes its name from the Swahili word, "pangani," meaning "place of enchantment." That's a lot more poetic than *Gorilla Falls Exploration Trail*,

Did You Know?

THE ORIGINAL CONCEPT FOR *THE BONEYARD* INCLUDED A ROLLER COASTER THAT WAS TO HAVE BEEN CALLED *THE EXCAVATOR*.

the trail's original name. "Rafiki" means "friend"; "anandapur" means "place of all delights"; "harambe" means "coming together."

23. c.) Forbidden Mountain
While many people believe that you are traveling through the legendary Mount Everest on your *Expedition Everest* adventure, you are actually part of the expedition on its way to that famous peak. Your steam train takes you from your base camp up and through the treacherous Forbidden Mountain, home of the mysterious Yeti, protector of the mountains.

24. a.) Flik
You will find one of Disney's finest 3-D attractions in the caverns of *The Tree of Life*. The show features characters from the film *A Bug's Life* and includes Audio-Animatronics, a 3-D motion picture . . . and a few surprises!

25. b.) DinoLand U.S.A.
DinoLand U.S.A., the funny, quirky area of DAK, currently contains seven attractions: *The Boneyard, Theater in the Wild* (former home of *Tarzan Rocks!*), *Primeval Whirl, TriceraTop Spin, Dino-Sue T-Rex, DINOSAUR,* and the *Fossil Fun Games.* Asia has a total of four, as does Rafiki's Planet Watch, while Africa has only two.

26. d.) *Maharajah Jungle Trek*
In this self-guided, walk-through attraction in Asia, you can wander through the ruins of an ancient temple and forest and meet their exotic inhabitants. Birds, giant fruit bats, Komodo dragons, antelopes, tigers, and many more await your gaze. Look closely and you'll also spot a number of "Hidden Mickeys."

27. b.) 14
At over 14 stories high, the majestic *Tree of Life* dominates the DAK skyline. It stretches over 165 feet across and has a trunk that is 50 feet in diameter. Like the Magic Kingdom's Cinderella Castle, *The Tree of Life* serves as a beautiful centerpiece to Animal Kingdom.

28. c.) The Discovery Network
The Discovery Network collaborated with Disney in journeys to China and the eastern Himalayas

for research for *Expedition Everest*. Accuracy was of paramount importance to the Imagineers, who spent years in Nepal and Tibet acquiring the knowledge and skills needed to achieve their goal: to create an experience that would immerse Guests in the culture and spirit of the region.

29. d.) *Mickey's Jingle Jungle Parade*

Celebrate the holiday season with Mickey and the gang plus puppets and floats in this daytime parade featuring holiday music with an international flair. It runs twice a day from November until early January.

30. b.) Fantasia Gardens

Located on what was to be the "good side" of this mythical land (as opposed to the "evil side" where you would find dragons and the like), "Fantasia Gardens" was a proposed boat ride through the classic animated film, *Fantasia*. Crocodiles, dancing hippos, centaurs, and fauns would be found in this musical attraction. Sadly, the entire concept for this area of the park appears to be

Did You Know?

DISNEY'S ANIMAL KINGDOM IS ACCREDITED BY THE AMERICAN ZOO AND AQUARIUM ASSOCIATION. SO MUCH FOR BEING "NAHTAZU"!

on indefinite hold, but Fantasia Gardens miniature golf course bears the name and features dancing hippos.

31. a.) Serka Zong
The mythical village of Serka Zong in *Expedition Everest* includes several buildings housing a hiking supply store, hotel, and even an "Internet Café." These structures were carefully constructed to reflect Nepalese architecture and styles accurately and convey the culture of Nepal. Disney Imagineers studied building materials and techniques in Nepal and Tibet, including what is known as "rammed earth" construction, in

which moist dirt is hammered with mallets until it reaches the proper consistency for building.

32. c.) Humans
According to Native American legend, there is only one animal with the power to save the forest, and *Pocahontas and Her Forest Friends* sets out to discover what it is. After Grandmother Willow tells her to ask the animals, Pocahontas questions the porcupine, possum, rabbit, and other creatures she meets along her way. Their answers lead us all to discover that only humans can save the forest.

Did You Know?

1,800 TONS OF STEEL WERE USED IN *EXPEDITION EVEREST*'S MOUNTAIN STRUCTURE. THAT IS ABOUT 6 TIMES THE AMOUNT THAT WOULD BE USED IN A TRADITIONAL OFFICE BUILDING OF THE SAME SIZE.

33. d.) Green
TriceraTop Spin, like *Dumbo* in the MK, is a "hub-and-spoke" ride. Up to four Guests ride in a green dinosaur that spins around a giant top (which opens to reveal a dinosaur!).

34. a.) A merry-go-round
While the majestic *Tree of Life* that sits as the focal point of DAK seems a natural for this animal-themed park, it was not part of the original design concept. Instead, Imagineers planned a gigantic carousel for the park's icon. That concept was dismissed, however, as too childish for the authentic atmosphere they were trying to create. And so, the idea for a tree was born . . . sort of. The park's lead Imagineer, Disney Legend Joe Rohde, wanted a "living" object as the centerpiece. He envisioned a 50-foot tree on which children could play. But that was too small in comparison to the other WDW park icons, such as *Spaceship Earth* in Epcot. So, they grew the tree on paper to 145 feet. But that created another problem: even a 14-story tree had to meet WDW's building codes, such as being able to withstand Florida's 90 mph hurricanes. Disney's initial solution wasn't to make a stronger tree, it was to shield it from the elements altogether by encasing it in a giant dome covered in fake plants. (Imagineers affectionately referred to this concept as the "Broccoli" phase.) Fortunately,

Animal Kingdom's construction manager made a connection between the tree's internal structure and oil rigs he remembered seeing in the Gulf of Mexico. He hired a Houston company to build a rig to a Disney engineer's specifications, and *The Tree of Life* took shape.

35. c.) *Flights of Wonder*
Flights of Wonder opened with DAK in 1998. In fact, it was the only attraction open in the park's Asia section for a number of months. The show has changed slightly over the years because it relies on live birds and some of its performers have "flown the coop." (Sorry — had to!)

36. a.) "When it comes to Safaris, we go WILD!"
Kilimanjaro Safaris, DAK's flagship attraction, takes you on a "journey through Africa's amazing wildlife." Look for gazelles, giraffes, zebras, ostriches, elephants, lions, and rhinos as your vehicle bumps along the dirt trails and over a creaky bridge.

37. b.) Time Rovers
DINOSAUR's Time Rovers are 12-passenger vehicles that take Guests back in time and WAY off the road! You can learn more about them in the pre-show from Dr. Marsh. They all bear the designation "CTX," paying homage to the attraction's former name, *Countdown To eXtinction*.

Did You Know?

A FAILED WAVE-MAKING MACHINE, BUILT OFF
THE SOUTHERN SHORE OF BEACHCOMBER ISLE
NEAR DISNEY'S POLYNESIAN RESORT, WAS SCUTTLED
ON THE BOTTOM OF THE SEVEN SEAS LAGOON.
WHILE ORIGINAL PLANS CALLED FOR THE MACHINE
TO MAKE WAVES LARGE ENOUGH FOR SURFING,
THE WAVES CAUSED SUCH BEACH EROSION
THAT THE MACHINE WAS SHUT DOWN.
IT NOW SERVES AS A REEF FOR FISH.

CHAPTER SIX

Beyond the Parks

1. Which of these hotels is located closest to the Magic Kingdom?
- a.) Disney's All Star-Music Resort
- b.) Disney's BoardWalk Villas
- c.) Disney's Wilderness Lodge
- d.) Disney's Fort Wilderness Resort & Campground

2. According to legend, what was the name of the fictional hurricane that created Typhoon Lagoon?
- a.) Tilly
- b.) Daisy
- c.) Connie
- d.) Valerie

3. About how many miles do the monorail tracks cover?
- a.) 14.7
- b.) 5.9
- c.) 29
- d.) 33

4. What nighttime show can be seen on the Seven Seas Lagoon and Bay Lake?

- a.) *Fantasmic!*
- b.) *SpectroMagic*
- c.) *Main Street Electrical Parade*
- d.) *Electrical Water Pageant*

5. Which of the following could you NOT see at Disney's Wide World of Sports?
- a.) Harlem Globetrotters training camp
- b.) Orlando Magic training camp
- c.) The NFL Quarterback Challenge
- d.) Atlanta Braves Spring Training

6. Where is the monorail track's highest point?
- a.) The circle around *Spaceship Earth* in Epcot
- b.) At the Grand Floridian station
- c.) Outside the Contemporary Resort
- d.) At the Transportation and Ticket Center

Did You Know?

IT WOULD TAKE 4,000 CDs TO FILL THE JUKEBOX IN THE "ROCK INN" AREA OF DISNEY'S ALL-STAR MUSIC RESORT. THAT'S ENOUGH TO PLAY FOR 135 DAYS WITHOUT HEARING THE SAME CD TWICE.

7. What was the original name of the Downtown Disney Marketplace?

    a.) Pleasure Island Marketplace

    b.) Lake Buena Vista Village

    c.) Walt Disney World Village

    d.) The name has never changed.

8. Which Disney Resort is located around a 15-acre lake?

    a.) Disney's Contemporary

    b.) Disney's Coronado Springs

    c.) Disney's Port Orleans – Riverside

    d.) Disney's BoardWalk Inn

9. Disney's Port Orleans Resorts are situated along the banks of the Sassagoula River. What does Sassagoula mean?

    a.) Sassagoula is the Indian word for "Mississippi."

    b.) Sassagoula is the original French name for the area in Louisiana where New Orleans is now located.

    c.) Sassagoula was the last name of one of Disney's Imagineers.

    d.) Sassagoula is a completely made-up word with no meaning.

10. How many cars are there in each monorail train?

    a.) 3

    b.) 4

    c.) 6

    d.) 7

11. Which of the following was never one of the names for the golf-themed hotel located near the Polynesian Resort?

    a.) The Disney Inn

    b.) Shades of Green

    c.) The Golf Resort

    d.) The Buena Vista Palace

12. What were the names of the side-wheeler steamboats that used

to transport Guests on the Seven Seas Lagoon and Bay Lake in the '70s and '80s?
a.) The Excursion Steamers
b.) The Liberty Belles
c.) The World Cruisers
d.) *Steamboat Willie* and *Steamboat Minnie*

13. In what year did Pleasure Island open?
a.) 1987
b.) 1989
c.) 1991
d.) 1993

14. What was the name of the hands-on educational resort located at WDW?
a.) The Disney Quest Villas
b.) Saratoga Springs Resort
c.) The Disney Imagineers Club
d.) The Disney Institute

15. Which of these Disney Resorts opened last?
a.) Beach Club Resort & Villas
b.) All-Star Movies
c.) Villas at Wilderness Lodge
d.) Coronado Springs

16. How many WDW restaurants have been awarded the exclusive AAA Five-Diamond Award?
a.) 0
b.) 1
c.) 2
d.) 3

17. What is the name of the golf course that winds through Disney's Old Key West Resort?
a.) Palm
b.) Magnolia
c.) Lake Buena Vista Golf Course
d.) Eagle Pines

18. Where can you find "Runoff Rapids"?
a.) Blizzard Beach
b.) Typhoon Lagoon
c.) *Splash Mountain*
d.) *Kali River Rapids*

19. What company built the original WDW monorails?
a.) Boeing
b.) Bombardier
c.) Martin Marietta
d.) WED Engineering

20. Which of these restaurants is NOT found in the Downtown Disney Marketplace?
a.) McDonald's
b.) Rainforest Café
c.) Cap'n Jack's Oyster Bar
d.) House of Blues

21. What is the name of the children's area at Typhoon Lagoon?
a.) Ketchakiddie Creek
b.) Nick's Nook
c.) Kiddie Cay
d.) Baby Bay

22. How many monorails were in operation on WDW's opening day in 1971?
a.) 1
b.) 3
c.) 9
d.) 12

23. What restaurant recommends that you "Live, Love, Eat"?
a.) Rainforest Café
b.) Bongo's Cuban Café
c.) House of Blues
d.) Wolfgang Puck Café

24. In what year did the Fort Wilderness Railroad cease operations?
a.) 1979
b.) 1981
c.) 1987
d.) 1998

25. Which is the most recent addition to Disney's All-Star Resorts?
a.) Music
b.) Sports
c.) Movies
d.) They all opened at the same time.

26. What is the name of the shipwrecked boat located at Disney's Yacht & Beach Club Resorts?
a.) *Miss Fortune*
b.) *Swallow*
c.) *Titus*
d.) *Albatross*

27. How many "official" hotels are located in Downtown Disney Hotel Plaza?
a.) None
b.) 3
c.) 5
d.) 7

28. What Disney artist designed the mosaic murals in the Grand Canyon Concourse of the

Did You Know?

THE ROLLING CHAIRS THAT TRAVEL ALONG DISNEY'S BOARDWALK COVER MORE MILES EVERY YEAR THAN THE DISTANCE BETWEEN CONEY ISLAND, NEW YORK, AND ATLANTIC CITY, NEW JERSEY.

Contemporary Hotel?
a.) Herb Ryman
b.) Sid Cahuenga
c.) Mary Blair
d.) John Hench

29. Which of these is NOT a room in the Adventurers Club?
a.) Treasure Room
b.) Library
c.) Music Room
d.) Mask Room

30. What special event at WDW includes a "Party for the Senses"?
a.) Flower and Garden Festival
b.) Holiday Splendor
c.) Night of Joy
d.) Food and Wine Festival

31. What is the name of the athletic stadium at Disney's Wide World of Sports?
a.) Heinz Field
b.) All Star Stadium
c.) Hess Field
d.) Cracker Jack Stadium

32. In what year was Disney's town of Celebration, Florida established?
a.) 1987
b.) 1989
c.) 1994
d.) 1996

33. What provided the inspiration for the theming of Saratoga Springs Resort?
a.) Polo
b.) Horse racing
c.) Pop culture
d.) Trains and railroads

34. WDW and magician David Copperfield worked together in the mid-1990s to develop which of the following for WDW?
a.) A roller coaster for Disney-MGM Studios
b.) A magic shop for Main Street, U.S.A.
c.) A magic training course at the Disney Institute
d.) A magic-themed restaurant for Downtown Disney

Did You Know?

U.S. STEEL, THE COMPANY THAT BUILT THE CONTEMPORARY AND POLYNESIAN RESORTS, HAD ORIGINALLY PLANNED ON OWNING AND RUNNING THEM. BUT ROY DISNEY DECIDED TO BUY THEM OUT AND LET DISNEY NOT ONLY OWN, BUT OPERATE, ITS HOTELS.

35. How many rooms does the WDW Swan have?
- a.) 111
- b.) 329
- c.) 758
- d.) 1,971

36. What is the name of the miniature golf course located next to Blizzard Beach?
- a.) Fantasia Gardens
- b.) Ice Gator Golf
- c.) Winter Summerland
- d.) Goofy Golf

37. If you boarded a boat at the Port Orleans – Riverside Resort, where could you end up?
- a.) Downtown Disney
- b.) The Transportation and Ticket Center
- c.) Magic Kingdom
- d.) Disney's BoardWalk

38. What is the largest resort on WDW property?
- a.) Disney's Grand Floridian Resort & Spa
- b.) Disney's Pop Century Resort
- c.) Disney's Animal Kingdom Lodge
- d.) Disney's Caribbean Beach Resort

39. The Empress Lilly riverboat, located in what is now Downtown Disney, originally contained three different restaurants. Which of these was NOT one of them?
- a.) Captain's Lounge
- b.) Steerman's Quarters
- c.) Empress Room
- d.) Fisherman's Deck

40. What was the Golf Resort originally planned to be?
- a.) Walt Disney's vacation home
- b.) A country club

Did You Know?

THE ORIGINAL MONORAIL LOOP — CONNECTING
THE TRANSPORTATION AND TICKET CENTER,
THE RESORT HOTELS, AND THE MAGIC KINGDOM —
CONSISTED OF 337 INDIVIDUAL TRACK BEAMS,
EACH OF WHICH WAS 85 TO 110 FEET LONG.
THEY WERE MADE OF CONCRETE WITH
A FOAMED POLYSTYRENE CORE TO LIGHTEN
THE WEIGHT TO A FEATHERY 55 TONS.

c.) An Asian-themed resort
d.) A men-only club

41. What is the name of the mountain in Typhoon Lagoon?
a.) Mount Kilimanjaro
b.) Mount Mayday
c.) Mount Mickey
d.) Summit Plummet

42. How much did the monorail track cost to build per mile?
a.) $100,000
b.) $500,000
c.) $1,000,000
d.) $1,500,000

43. What is the main building of the Polynesian Resort called?
a.) The South Pacific Reception Hall
b.) The Great Ceremonial House
c.) Tonga House
d.) Rapa Nui Reception Hall

44. Which of these Disney Resorts opened first?
a.) Grand Floridian Resort & Spa
b.) All-Star Sports
c.) Wilderness Lodge
d.) Old Key West

45. What's the name of Blizzard Beach's mascot?
a.) Slushy
b.) Ketchakiddie
c.) Frosty
d.) Ice Gator

46. In which World Showcase country did *Cirque du Soleil* originate?
a.) Canada
b.) France
c.) United States
d.) England

47. Which of the following was NOT a name for one of the types of villas near the Walt Disney World Village?
a.) Treehouse Villas
b.) Fairway Villas
c.) Vacation Villas
d.) Resort Villas

48. What did the Wildhorse Saloon replace?
a.) 8 TRAX
b.) The Neon Armadillo
c.) The Fireworks Factory
d.) XZFR Rockin' Rollerdrome

49. How tall are the statues atop the WDW Swan and Dolphin hotels?
a.) 9 feet tall
b.) 18 feet tall
c.) 3 stories tall
d.) 5 stories tall

50. What is the name of the sea serpent constructed of LEGO bricks in the Downtown Disney lagoon?
a.) Brickley
b.) Legosaurus
c.) Ogel
d.) Pete

THE ANSWERS
TO CHAPTER SIX

1. c.) Disney's Wilderness Lodge
Wilderness Lodge is modeled after the old National Park lodges found in Yellowstone Park. It even has its own geyser, as well as a spring that "originates" in the lobby. One of Disney's Deluxe Resorts, the 728-room lodge is surrounded by pine, cypress, and oak forests. It is located on the shores of Bay Lake, close to the Magic Kingdom.

2. c.) Connie
Hurricane Connie, the storm that turned the "Placid Palms Resort"

into Typhoon Lagoon, is the same fictional storm that wreaked havoc on Pleasure Island back in its pre-club days. In fact, pieces of debris from Pleasure Island can be found on Typhoon Lagoon, including the signature ship, the *Miss Tilly*, and boxes from the old Fireworks Factory (which at one time was the name of a Pleasure Island restaurant).

3. a.) 14.7
From early morning until long after the theme parks close, the WDW monorail system transports Guests

between the transportation hub and three resort hotels as well as between the Magic Kingdom and Epcot. If you add up all the trips the monorails have made over the 14.7 mile (23.7 km) track since 1971, the mileage logged would be equal to more than 25 round trips to the moon — even taking into consideration that the original monorail route was a bit shorter (it was extended in 1981 in preparation for the opening of Epcot). The original fleet was retired and replaced in 1990.

4. d.) *Electrical Water Pageant*

The *Electrical Water Pageant* is one of WDW's longest-running shows. The show, performed nightly on Bay Lake and the Seven Seas Lagoon, includes over 1,000 feet of sparkling sea creature floats shaped like dolphins, dragons, and sea monsters. The floating parade ends with a patriotic salute to America. The show can be seen from the Polynesian, Grand Floridian, and Contemporary resorts, as well as Wilderness Lodge and Fort Wilderness.

5. b.) Orlando Magic training camp

Guests can watch athletes compete in their favorite sports at Wide World of Sports' beautiful state-of-the-art facilities. Teams such as the Super Bowl XXXVII Champion Tampa Bay Buccaneers, Atlanta Braves, Harlem Globetrotters, and Orlando Rays (the AA affiliate of the Tampa Bay Devil Rays) train and play there.

6. c.) Outside the Contemporary Resort

As the monorail approaches the Contemporary, it reaches its highest elevation of 65 feet.

7. b.) Lake Buena Vista Village

"Lake Buena Vista Village" was the name of the Downtown Disney Marketplace when it opened on March 22, 1975. It was next "The Walt Disney World Village," before becoming "The Disney Village Marketplace" in 1989. It got its current name, "Downtown Disney Marketplace," in 1997. Throughout its identity crisis, it has been home to numerous restaurants and shops

Did You Know?

THE FANTASIA POOL AT DISNEY'S
ALL-STAR MOVIES RESORT HAS, OH,
JUST ABOUT 231,610 GALLONS OF
WATER IN IT.

— and even a liquor store, Village Spirits. (After 7 days of running around in the Florida heat with five screaming kids and a maxed-out credit card, you'd need a drink, too!)

8. b.) Disney's Coronado Springs Resort
Coronado Springs is a Moderate Resort, themed to resemble Mexico and the American Southwest. It is also one of WDW's largest resorts, with 1,967 rooms separated into three regions: the Casitas (marked by plazas and fountains); the Ranchos (featuring a rocky, dry creek bed known as an arroyo); and the Cabanas (which call to mind Mexico's beautiful coastal areas). The entire resort is set around a 15-acre lake known as "Lago Dorado" (or "Golden Lake"). The 0.9-mile Esplanade circling the lake is the perfect path for leisurely strolls or bike rides, and you can rent kayaks, Water Mice, and canopy boats on the lagoon.

9. a.) Sassagoula is the Indian word for "Mississippi."

The Sassagoula River runs from Downtown Disney, near Disney's Old Key West Resort, where it connects to the Trumbo Canal, past the rear of Disney's Port Orleans – French Quarter, and into the center of Port Orleans – Riverside, where it encircles Ol' Man Island.

10. c.) 6
Every Mark VI monorail train consists of six cars, each with an overall length of 203 feet, 6 inches and an overall height of 10 feet, 5.5 inches. Every car is air-conditioned, has 124 tires, and can carry 360 passengers (Mickey Mouse stuffed dolls not included).

11. d.) The Buena Vista Palace
The original "Golf Resort" was renamed the "Disney Inn" in February 1986. It subsequently became the military-only "Shades of Green" in February of 1994. The 875-room Buena Vista Palace Resort and Spa is located near Downtown Disney. It changed its name to the Wyndham Palace Resort and Spa in November

1998, but reverted to its original name in 2005.

12. a.) The Excursion Steamers

Two side-wheel Excursion Steamers, the *Southern Seas* and the *Ports O' Call*, once transported Guests to and from the Magic Kingdom on Bay Lake and the Seven Seas Lagoon. They were later used for pleasure cruises, including moonlight cruises with full bar service. The "original" *Southern Seas* was forced into retirement in 1977, after sinking during routine maintenance. It is rumored that many of the pieces from the ship can be found around WDW, most noticeably in Typhoon Lagoon. The replacement *Southern Seas* and the *Ports O' Call* were retired for good in later years.

13. b.) 1989

Pleasure Island opened on May 1, 1989. Created for grown-ups and located in Downtown Disney, the six-acre man-made island contains shops, restaurants, and (mainly) adults-only nightclubs. It parties late into the evening, with something for everyone, from comedy and R&B to rock and high-energy dancing. Back then, entry to all of the clubs, restaurants, and shops cost less than $10. You'll pay over $20 now.

14. d.) The Disney Institute

The Disney Institute, located on the shores of Lake Buena Vista, stood across from the area currently known as Downtown Disney Marketplace. It was a unique resort in that it offered more than 80 different educational programs for both mind and body. The Institute provided hands-on learning vacation programs in subjects such as Animation, Cooking, Gardening, Television Production, and more. The campus contained only 457 rooms and was designed to look like a small town, complete with a welcome center, performance hall, sports center, spa, cinema, and 28 workshops and studios. The Institute was the brainchild of Michael Eisner and his wife, Jane, who were inspired to open it after visiting the Chautauqua Institution in upstate New York. Unfortunately, though, even after years of testing and market research, Disney had to learn the hard way that most people don't want to go to school while they're on vacation. The

Did You Know?

THE FIRST WEDDING
IN DISNEY'S WEDDING
PAVILION WAS TELEVISED
LIVE JUNE 18, 1995, ON
LIFETIME TELEVISION AS
PART OF ITS *WEDDINGS
OF A LIFETIME* SERIES.

Institute closed in 2002 and was
torn down to make way for a new
Disney Vacation Club (DVC) resort.

15. a.) Beach Club Resort & Villas
The Resorts opened as follows:
1997 - Coronado Springs Resort
1999 - All-Star Movies Resort
2000 - Villas of Wilderness Lodge
2002 - Beach Club Resort & Villas

16. b.) 1
Victoria & Albert's at Disney's
Grand Floridian Resort & Spa
received the AAA Five-Diamond
Award after 10 years of excellence
at the four-diamond level. It is the
only restaurant in Central Florida
to earn this prestigious distinction,
which AAA says is awarded only to
establishments that exemplify an
impeccable standard of excellence.

17. c.) Lake Buena Vista Golf Course
Located near Downtown Disney
Marketplace, the Lake Buena Vista
Golf Course winds through the Old
Key West Resort and what was once
the Disney Institute. The course
was designed by Joe Lee in a classic
country club style and is laced with
a combination of dense pine forests,
Disney resort properties, and well-
bunkered greens to present quite a
challenge. It has hosted a PGA Tour,
an LPGA Tour, and a USGA event.
The Palm and Magnolia courses are
located near the Shades of Green and
Polynesian Resorts. Eagle Pines is
located near three resorts: Fort Wilderness, Port Orleans–Riverside, and
Saratoga Springs (the newest Disney
Vacation Club Resort).

18. a.) Blizzard Beach
Runoff Rapids is a three-story high
inner-tube water slide in which
Guests plummet down one of three
different twisting, turning flumes.

For added excitement, one of the flumes is completely dark inside!

19. c.) Martin Marietta

The Mark IV trains used in WDW when the resort opened in 1971 were built by Martin Marietta. They were designed in Burbank, California and built in Orlando. They operated at the Resort for 18 years, carrying more than 250 million Guests to and from the parks. Alweg Company of Cologne, Germany, built the original Disneyland monorail.

20. d.) House of Blues

Downtown Disney Marketplace is home to almost 20 different places to grab a bite, from full-service dining to candy shops and fast food. But the House of Blues isn't among them. It's located on Downtown Disney's West Side.

21. a.) Ketchakiddie Creek

If you're between two and five years old, then Ketchakiddie Creek at Typhoon Lagoon water park is for you! Here, you'll find pint-sized slides, geysers, and fountains for you and your parents (whom you have to bring along with you) to enjoy!

22. b.) 3

Monorails Orange, Green, and Gold were in service on opening day. They were delivered to the park at the rate of one per month between April and June 1971. They were followed by Monorail Blue (in service October 20, 1971), Monorail Red (in service November 7), and Monorail Yellow (in service December 3). Monorails Pink, Silver, Purple, and Black followed, entering service between July 3 and December 22, 1972. The last two trains delivered were Lime and Coral, in 1977, which were eventually sold to Bally's in Las Vegas for use on its new monorail line (they have since been removed from service).

23. d.) Wolfgang Puck Café

Located in Downtown Disney – West Side, the Wolfgang Puck Café serves up the legendary chef's world famous California-style cuisine in a two-story, 18,000-square-foot restaurant. The building actually houses four different dining options: Wolfgang Puck Café, Wolfgang Puck Express, B's Bar, and The Dining Room. They all embody the owner's philosophy of "live, love, eat," offering brightly colored, high-energy dining experiences with reasonably priced menu choices to satisfy and delight any palette.

24. a.) 1979

Although a *Fort Wilderness Railroad* was planned for the Fort Wilderness Resort and Campground (one of WDW's original three resorts) from the start, it was not installed for almost two years. The railroad, also known as the *Wilderness Line Railway*, ran from 1974 until 1979, offering Guests a unique mode of transportation through the large campground. Although somewhat similar in appearance to the *WDW Railroad*, the Fort Wilderness trains were much smaller (4/5 scale engines and coaches) and were designed and built by Walt Disney Productions specifically for WDW by MAPO, Disney's Glendale, California, manufacturing arm, while its Buena

Vista Construction company laid the three and a half miles of 30-inch-gauge track. In 1973, the trains were transported on flatbed trucks to Florida, where they and the tracks underwent testing before the line opened in 1974.

25. c.) Movies

Disney's All-Star Movies Resort opened in January 1999. Ground breaking took place in 1997, and the resort started taking reservations in January 1998. Like the other two All-Star hotels, All-Star Movies features 1,920 rooms and falls into the "Value" price range. All-Star Sports opened April 29, 1994, All-Star Music in November 1994.

26. d.) *Albatross*

The shipwrecked craft at the Yacht & Beach Club Resorts is known as the *Albatross*. In fact, kids can take an "Albatross Treasure Cruise" and travel the waters of Crescent Lake and the Epcot World Showcase Lagoon in search of buried treasure.

27. d.) 7

Situated inside the Walt Disney World Resort (or "on property," as Disney puts it) the following seven hotels are just a short walk from Downtown Disney and Pleasure Island and offer free bus service to the theme parks on a regular schedule. One even hosts Character Meals. However, unlike the Disney resort hotels, they are not owned and operated by Disney. The hotels are:

1. Best Western Lake Buena Vista Resort
2. Buena Vista Palace and Spa
3. Doubletree Guest Suites Resort
4. Grosvenor Resort (hosts Character Meals)
5. Hilton in the Walt Disney World® Resort
6. Holiday Inn
7. Hotel Royal Plaza

28. c.) Mary Blair
Mary Blair's largest mural is located in the Grand Canyon Concourse of the Contemporary Resort hotel. Featuring birds, animals, flowers, a five-legged goat, and American Indian children, the mural consists of 18,000 hand-painted tiles and is 90 feet high.

29. c.) Music Room
Themed as a 1937 club for gentlemen explorers, The Adventurers Club includes four different rooms: the Main Room/Parlor (where you learn and sing the Club's oath), the Mask Room, the Treasure Room (look for Beezle the Genie), and the infamous Library, where the main shows take place. Kungaloosh!

30. d.) Food and Wine Festival
Guests can taste fine wine and paired cuisine during Epcot's annual Food and Wine Festival,

held from October through November. Live entertainment, cooking demonstrations, seminars, and more complement the food offerings. Epcot's Flower and Garden Festival takes place every spring. Magic Kingdom hosts "Night of Joy," featuring contemporary Christian musicians, for two nights in September. All four theme parks join in WDW's holiday celebration, held from Thanksgiving to New Year's Day.

31. d.) Cracker Jack Stadium
Located near Disney's Animal Kingdom, the stadium (formerly known as Disney Field) is part of Disney's 220-acre Wide World of Sports. This Spanish Mission-design stadium is the tallest of all the Major League Baseball spring training sites. It offers good sightlines with classic charm: 80 percent of its 7,500 seats are located between first and third bases. Cracker Jack is currently the spring training home of the Atlanta Braves.

32. c.) 1994
Celebration is an innovative, pedestrian-friendly town that successfully promotes a strong sense of community. Themed to resemble a small southeastern town with pre-1940s architecture, it was established in

1994 and the first residents moved in June 18, 1996. In many ways the town fulfills Walt Disney's dream of a planned community in Walt Disney World, offering its residents a business district, schools, entertainment, and an impressive, state-of-the-art hospital. It is located just a few miles from WDW.

33. b.) Horse racing
The 552-room Saratoga Springs Resort & Spa features Victorian architecture influenced by the sport of horse racing. Located across the lake from Downtown Disney, the resort is modeled after late nineteenth century New York state country retreats.

34. d.) A magic-themed restaurant for Downtown Disney
In 1996, David Copperfield announced plans for "Copperfield's Magic Underground," an interactive magic-themed restaurant to be located in WDW, with another to be built in New York's Times Square.

He and Disney proposed to take patrons to "the secret underground lair of David Copperfield" on a magic adventure where they will actually "experience the magic" (such as levitating tables) as they dine. While the restaurant, set to open in the summer of 1999, never "materialized" (pardon the pun), a store bearing the same name was located for a brief time in Downtown Disney's West Side.

35. c.) 758
Located between Epcot and Disney-MGM Studios, the 12-story WDW Swan and neighboring WDW Dolphin were designed by noted architect Michael Graves. The two share a three-acre grotto swimming pool and a white-sand beach and, together, offer their guests a total of three lap pools, two tennis courts, a spa, a supervised children's program, and 17 places to grab a bite, with Character Dining in one of them. The Dolphin offers many more

Did You Know?
CHEF MICKEY'S SERVES 4,000 EGGS, 1,700 MICKEY-SHAPED WAFFLES, AND 1,500 PANCAKES EVERY DAY AT BREAKFAST.

guest rooms, however, 1509 to the Swan's 758.

36. c.) Winter Summerland

This 36-hole miniature golf course is located near the entrance to Disney's Blizzard Beach water park and is divided into two courses, Winter and Summer (or Snow and Sand). The Winter course has the same look as Blizzard Beach, while the Summer course has a tropical holiday theme. Winter Summerland is the second themed miniature golf course at WDW, following in the success of Fantasia Gardens.

37. a.) Downtown Disney

One benefit of staying at the Port Orleans Resorts is the luxury of being able to take a leisurely, free 20-minute cruise down the Sassagoula River to the Downtown Disney Marketplace.

38. b.) Disney's Pop Century Resort

Located near Disney's Wide World of Sports complex, this value resort includes 2,880 rooms, two 5,000-square-foot arcades, eight courtyards, six pools, two playgrounds, an area for shopping and dining, and recreational paths for bike riding around Hourglass Lake — and it's not even finished. The resort is being constructed in two phases and will ultimately have 5,760 rooms spread across 20 buildings. Phase I, "The

Classic Years," opened on December 14, 2003. Completion of Phase II, "The Legendary Years," has yet to be scheduled.

39. a.) Captain's Lounge

Named for Walt Disney's wife, Lillian, the *Empress Lilly* riverboat opened in 1977 on the shore of Lake Buena Vista. Offering the most elegant dining in Walt Disney World Village (and possibly all of WDW up until the opening of Victoria & Albert's in the Grand Floridian), it provided multiple dining options. It also included one of the first Character Breakfasts in WDW. This tribute to an 1880's Mississippi stern-wheeler contained not only the restaurants, but also small Victorian lounges and a lounge for an after-dinner show and cocktails. The Fisherman's Deck offered seafood with a wonderful view of Lake Buena Vista. The Steerman's Quarters, a dinner-only restaurant, was renowned for its Angus beef. The Empress Room was the flagship four-star restaurant, and the Baton Rouge Lounge offered drinks, music, and light dining options. On April 22, 1995, the *Empress Lilly* closed for refurbishment. Its original rear paddlewheel was removed, and it reopened as Fulton's Crab House.

40. b.) A country club
The Golf Resort Hotel, located on 400 acres near the Polynesian Resort, was originally planned as a country club where Guests could play golf, eat, and socialize, but would have no overnight accommodations.

Guest rooms were added in 1973 to make it a complete resort. The name was changed to The Disney Inn in 1986, and then to Shades of Green in 1994, when the U.S. Department of Defense leased the hotel from Disney for its exclusive use. The DOD purchased the property outright on January 12, 1996. Shades of Green is presently the only Armed Forces Recreation Center in the continental U.S.

41. b.) Mount Mayday
The centerpiece of Typhoon Lagoon is the 100-foot tall Mount Mayday, which is surrounded by a 2.75 million-gallon wave pool.

42. c.) $1,000,000
Believe it or not, each and every mile of the WDW monorail track

cost an average of one million dollars to build, due in part to Disney's need for very quiet operation and fairly narrow, maintenance-free beams that would allow the monorail to run through the interior of its Contemporary Resort. The monorails run on rubber tires on a "track" that is actually a 26-inch-wide concrete beam with a foamed polystyrene core wrapped by steel and concrete. Each of the more than 400 beams was specifically designed for its location on the track, so that the track could conform to the land. The beams, which were built in Oregon and trucked to Florida, are supported by tapered concrete columns, spaced 110 feet apart. The columns feed electricity to a bar beneath the beams, which in turn powers the trains.

43. b.) The Great Ceremonial House

Disney's Polynesian Resort was one of two resorts that opened with the Magic Kingdom on October 1, 1971. The Great Ceremonial House is its main reception area. It features restaurants, shops, and a three-story high garden containing more than 75 varieties of tropical and subtropical plants. A monorail station and bus stop are just outside.

44. a.) Grand Floridian Resort & Spa

The deluxe Grand Floridian opened in July 1988 as the "Grand Floridian Beach Resort," WDW's fifth resort hotel, while the lakeside Old Key West opened in '91 as the first of Disney's Vacation Club Resorts (in fact, it was called "Disney's Vacation Club Resort" then and renamed in '96). The All-Star Sports value resort opened on April 29, 1994, followed a month later by the deluxe 728-room Wilderness Lodge on May 28. The GF became "Disney's Grand Floridian Resort & Spa" in the fall of 1997.

45. d.) Ice Gator

As "legend" has it, Blizzard Beach was created by a freak winter storm that dropped snow over the western side of the WDW. Here Disney built Florida's very first (and only) ski resort! However, the temperature began to rise, and as the snow melted, it began to pour down Mount Gushmore. Just when it looked like the new resort was a huge disaster, the now-famous blue "Ice Gator" was seen sliding down the slope, and "Blizzard Beach" was born! (Ever seen a blue alligator on skis?)

46. a.) Canada

Cirque du Soleil (or "Circus of the Sun") was formed in 1984 by a troupe of street performers known as "Le Club des Talons Hauts" (the high-heels club) who wanted to promote circus arts and street performance. Just 73 people worked

Did You Know?

THE TWO 55-FOOT TOTEM POLES IN THE WILDERNESS LODGE, THE EAGLE AND THE RAVEN, WERE CARVED IN WASHINGTON STATE.

for the company in its first year of existence. Today, *Cirque du Soleil* has more than 10 productions running on 3 continents and over 2,500 employees (with an average age of just 24)! Since its founding, more than 37,000,000 people have seen *Cirque*'s amazing performances.

47. d.) Resort Villas
In January 1972, the Disney Village Resorts opened near the shopping area known as Lake Buena Vista Village (which became the Walt Disney World Village in 1977). Known, as of 1985, as the Village Resort, the property was originally intended to be part of a residential community. (Yes, believe it or not, at one time there were plans to have permanent residences on WDW property. That's right — you could have lived *in* Walt Disney World had they come to pass!) The Village Resort was comprised of five types of properties: Club Lake Villas (which opened in 1980 and became known as "Club Suites" in 1989, and then "Club Bungalows" in 1996); Vacation Villas (later known as the "Townhouses"); Treehouse Villas; Fairway Villas, and four Grand Vista Homes. The Villas became part of the Disney Institute on February 9, 1996. Some have since been replaced by the first phase of the Saratoga Springs Resort, a Disney Vacation Club time-share property.

48. c.) The Fireworks Factory

The Fireworks Factory was a fun BBQ restaurant located in Pleasure Island. According to Disney legend, it got its name from the fireworks factory that Merriweather Pleasure, the adventurer who once owned the island, operated here until his cigar caused a huge explosion. When WDW's Pleasure Island was established, the charred remains of the factory became the appropriately named Fireworks Factory restaurant. The Factory was transformed first into the "Wildhorse Saloon" in May 1998 (adding country music and dance to the BBQ) and then, in 2001, into "Motion," a top 40 and alternative dance club.

49. d.) 5 stories tall

Five-story swan and dolphin statues rest atop the magnificent WDW Swan and Dolphin hotel buildings. The 26-story Dolphin is easily recognizable because of its central pyramidal roof, adorned with two dolphins 55 feet high. Across the lake from it, the 12-story Swan is topped with a pair of 47-foot swans.

50. a.) Brickley

Brickley, whose name was chosen from Guest and Cast Member entries in a naming contest, is made up of over one million LEGO bricks. The friendly sea serpent can be found outside the LEGO Imagination Center at Downtown Disney Marketplace.

INDEX

We use the following abbreviations:

AK – Disney's Animal Kingdom
DD – Downtown Disney
DM – Disney-MGM Studios
E – Epcot   R – Resort

FW – Fort Wilderness
MK – Magic Kingdom
P – Pleasure Island
WP – WDW Water Park

215

X Y Z